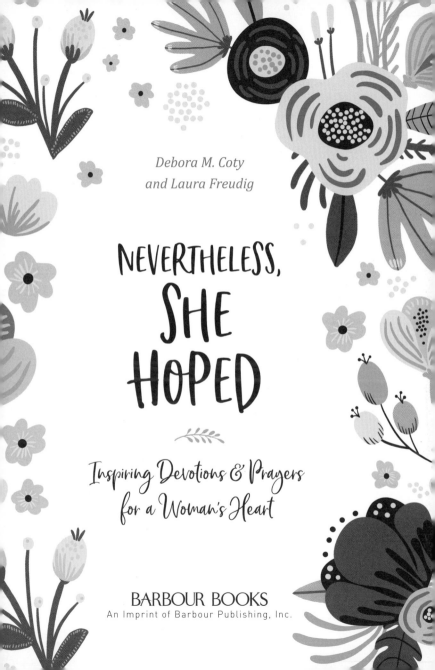

Debora M. Coty
and Laura Freudig

NEVERTHELESS, SHE HOPED

Inspiring Devotions & Prayers for a Woman's Heart

BARBOUR BOOKS
An Imprint of Barbour Publishing, Inc.

ISBN 978-1-64352-644-7

Published by Barbour Books, an imprint of Barbour Publishing, Inc., 1810 Barbour Drive, Uhrichsville, Ohio 44683, www.barbourbooks.com

Our mission is to inspire the world with the life-changing message of the Bible.

 Member of the
Evangelical Christian
Publishers Association

Printed in China.

NEVERTHELESS, HAVE HOPE!

Now may our Lord Jesus Christ Himself and God our Father,
who has loved us and given us eternal comfort and good
hope by grace, comfort and strengthen your hearts.
2 Thessalonians 2:16–17 nasb

Hope isn't just an emotion; it's a perspective, a discipline, a way of life. Hope is a journey of choice. For believers, hope is vital to a dynamic, thriving faith. . .one of the big three that will remain to the end of time: faith, hope, and love (1 Corinthians 13:13).

There are nineteen Hebrew translations of "hope" in the Old Testament alone, including trust, security, refuge, confidence, and shelter. Hope in Abba Father—our Papa God—is all of those qualities rolled into one life-changing bundle. There's no real living without it.

Hope is a glimmer in the darkness, the buttercup lifting its delicate head from a charred field, that supernatural nudge to persevere when all seems lost. Hope, dear sisters, is simply Jesus. I pray that you find Him in these pages.

DANCING iN THE PUDDLES

And so, Lord, where do I put my hope?
My only hope is in you.
Psalm 39:7 nlt

They say you can tell a lot about a person's foundation of hope by the way she handles a rainy day. Does she turn into a gloomy Gussy, wailing "Oh, woe is me. . ." or does she make the best of a bad situation? A hope-filled person will realize that abundant life in Christ isn't about simply enduring the storm but also about learning to dance in the puddles. So grab your galoshes, and let's boogie!

Dear Father, we want only sunny days, but without
rain the earth would be dry and lifeless. We thank You
for giving us exactly what we need, even when we think we
need something else. Help us to take what You give with
joy and dance in Your life-giving puddles! Amen.

WALKING FAITH

"Be strong and courageous, and act; do not fear
nor be dismayed, for the Lord God, my God, is with
you. He will not fail you nor forsake you."

1 Chronicles 28:20 nasb

What a life verse! What a creed to live by! We are assured that our God will never leave us or forsake us. We draw strength and courage from this assurance and are then able to *act*; to share our faith boldly—without fear—because we are never alone. The Lord God—*our* God—is with us.

Lord, Your promises give life—they are life. Thank You
for promising never to fail or forsake us. Thank You for
being the source of our strength and courage. Give us
the faith to live without fear in the light of Your
promises. In Your precious Name, amen.

SHOUTS OF JOY

He will yet fill your mouth with laughter
and your lips with shouts of joy.
JOB 8:21 NIV

Do you remember the last time you laughed till you cried? For many of us, it's been far too long. Stress tends to steal our joy, leaving us humorless and oh-so-serious. But lightness and fun haven't disappeared forever. They may be buried beneath the snow of a long, wintery life season, but spring is coming, girls. Laughter will bloom again, and our hearts will soar as our lips shout with joy. Grasp that hope!

Dear Lord, help us look actively for moments of joy—
not just the hollow, fleeting joys the world offers, but the true,
lasting, eternal joys that come only from You. Help us keep
our eyes looking in the right direction: fixed on Jesus
and the joy set before Him. Amen.

INTERIOR DECORATOR

You, O Lord, are a shield about me,
my glory, and the One who lifts my head.

Psalm 3:3 nasb

Have you ever caught a glimpse of yourself reflected in a window and were shocked at the hangdog image you unwittingly portrayed? Slumped shoulders, drooping head, defeated expression? You can straighten your posture and adjust your face, but if the change doesn't come from the inside out, it won't stick. God is our Interior Decorator. Only He can provide that inner joy that projects outward and lifts our heads. Invite Him in to work on your place.

Gracious Lord, we invite You into our hearts where You belong. Thank You for reminding us—when we would think little of ourselves—that we are daughters of the King! Remind us daily of the truth of the Gospel—that we were precious enough to die for. And let that show on our faces. Amen.

DESIGNER LABEL

We wish that each of you would always be eager to
show how strong and lasting your hope really is.
Hebrews 6:11 cev

Our behavior is always on display and, like it or not, we are judged by our actions. . .and inactions. Without an explanation for our behavior—that we're motivated by faith to be Christlike—people will make up their own ideas: *Her mama taught her right; she was just born nice; she acts sweet so everyone will like her.* Isn't it better to be up-front and give credit to the One we're emulating? Wear the label of your Designer proudly.

Lord, we don't want to be just nice people. We're not nice
people; we're sinners saved from God's wrath by the sacrifice
of His only Son. If that fires our hearts with thankfulness, it
should also loosen our lips. Help us to speak Your precious
name to those who so desperately need to hear it. Amen.

I'M NO EEYORE

Then [Job's] wife said to him, "Do you still hold
fast your integrity? Curse God and die!"
JOB 2:9 NASB

Job's wife was the unwilling recipient of Satan's attacks because of her husband's righteous life. When the going got tough, our girl lost faith and hope disintegrated. We too sometimes lose sight of all God has done for us and focus only on what He *didn't* do. Our attitudes nosedive and negativity imprisons us. Job's response is the key to escaping the shackles of Eeyore-ism: "I *know* that my Redeemer lives" (Job 19:25 NASB, emphasis added).

Father, when life gets hard, help us to cling
even tighter to You. There is no other rock, no other
Redeemer, no other strong tower, no other provider,
no other sustainer, no other Savior. You are all that
and more. In thanksgiving and faith, amen.

INSIDE-OUT LOVE

God has made everything beautiful for its own time.
ECCLESIASTES 3:11 NLT

Beauty is a concern of every woman to some degree. We worry about hair, make-up, weight, fashions. But real beauty can only come from God's inside-out love. Once we are able to finally comprehend His infinite and extravagant love for us—despite our flat feet and split ends—our heart-glow will reflect radiant beauty from the inside out. Only when we feel truly loved are we free to be truly lovely.

Dear Lord, our hearts are often beyond our own comprehension. But they are not beyond Yours, for You made us. Open our ears to the lies we are believing when we think we are not beautiful; open our eyes to the false images we are worshipping. In Jesus' Name, amen.

CONFOUNDED CORSETS

Cultivate inner beauty, the gentle,
gracious kind that God delights in.
1 PETER 3:4 MSG

In our quest for beauty, we buy into all sorts of crazy things: mud facials, cosmetic surgery, body piercings, obsessive dieting, squeezing size 10 feet into size 8 shoes. The image of Scarlett O'Hara's binding corset makes us shudder. (Reminds me of a pair of jeans I wrestled with just last week.) Yet God's idea of beauty is on the *inside*—where spandex cannot touch. Let's resolve to devote more time pursuing inner beauty that will never require Botox.

Dear Lord, I need to be reminded daily of the kind
of beauty that delights You. That knowledge is something
I can't find on television, on Facebook, or in a magazine.
I long to be beautiful in Your sight, and that beauty
secret is found only in Your Word. Amen.

GOOD ENOUGH

*Leah's eyes were weak, but Rachel
was beautiful of form and face.*
GENESIS 29:17 NASB

Have you ever felt like a booby prize?

No doubt Leah did. Hunky Jacob labored seven years to marry Leah's gorgeous sister, Rachel. Then their squirrelly father switched his daughters at the altar. Jacob freaked. Leah tanked. We too sometimes feel that we're not good enough; that we don't measure up. But Leah gave birth to six of the twelve tribes of Israel, the cornerstone of Judeo-Christendom.

God has a mighty plan for all of us Leahs.

*Dear God, thank You that You have a plan for each of us.
All the aspects of our forms, faces, and families were ordained
by You for Your purposes. Help us to give thanks for what
You have done, even if we don't yet understand the
story You are telling through our lives. Amen.*

GRANTER of DREAMS

Hope deferred makes the heart sick,
but a dream fulfilled is a tree of life.
PROVERBS 13:12 NLT

As a teenager, I dreamed of one day writing a book. But life intervened, and I became a wife, mother, occupational therapist, and piano teacher. My writing dream was shelved. Twenty-five years later, after my youngest chick flew the coop, God's still, small voice whispered, "It's time." Within five years, the Granter of Dreams delivered over seventy articles and nine book contracts.

What's your dream? Be brave and take the first step.

Lord, it amazes me how You see my heart and my
deepest dreams and work to fulfill them. I do not deserve
Your constant care and attention, and it boggles my mind
that the Creator of the universe has His eye on me.
Thank You, Lord. Thank You! Amen.

EVERYDAY BLESSINGS

But the eyes of the LORD are on those who fear him,
on those whose hope is in his unfailing love.

PSALM 33:18 NIV

The Lord of all creation is watching our every moment and wants to fill us with His joy. He often interrupts our lives with His blessings: butterflies dancing in sunbeams, dew-touched spiderwebs, cotton candy clouds, and glorious crimson sunsets. The beauty of His creation reassures us of His unfailing love and fills us with hope. But it is up to us to take the time to notice.

Dear Father, it's almost as though You are saying in those small moments, "Here I am. This is all for You. Look at how much I love You." Help us to hear Your voice and notice Your gifts and pour back praises to You. Amen.

STOP THE ROLLER COASTER

Why am I discouraged? Why is my heart so sad?
I will put my hope in God! I will praise him
again—my Savior and my God!

PSALM 43:5 NLT

For women, ruts of depression are often caused by careening hormones. Rampaging hormones can cause us to spend countless hours weeping without knowing why–or bite someone's head off, lose precious sleep, or sprout funky nervous habits. Knowing that this hormonally-crazed state is only temporary, we must intentionally place our hope in tomorrow and pray that God will turn the downside up!

Dear Lord, I pray that when my own body seems to be leading
my mind astray, I would turn to You to be my steady anchor in
the storm raging inside of me. I know I can't do this in my
own power, but Your Spirit living within me can. Amen.

MY REFUGE

God is our refuge and strength,
always ready to help in times of trouble.
Psalm 46:1 nlt

What is your quiet place? The place you go to get away from the fray, to chill out, think, regroup, and gain perspective? Mine is a hammock nestled beneath a canopy of oaks in my backyard . . .nobody around but birds, squirrels, an occasional wasp, God, and me. There I can pour out my heart to my Lord, *hear* His comforting voice, and *feel* His strength refresh me. We all need a quiet place. God, our refuge, will meet us there.

Dear Lord, I thank You for allowing me to have a peaceful
place to draw near to You. I realize what a gift that is and
how many people around the world have no such safe haven.
Thank You for being so good to me in this way. Amen.

A LiTTLE GOES A LONG WAY

The LORD our God has allowed a
few of us to survive as a remnant.

EZRA 9:8 NLT

Remnants. Useless by most standards, aren't they? But God is in the business of using tiny slivers of what's left to do mighty things. In the passage above, Nehemiah rebuilt the fallen walls of Jerusalem with a remnant of Israel; Noah's three sons repopulated the earth after the flood; four slave boys—Daniel, Shadrach, Meshach, and Abednego—kept faith alive for an entire nation. When it feels as if bits and pieces are all that has survived of your hope, remember how *much* God can accomplish with remnants!

Dear God, we are believers now because people in the
past held on to their faith despite opposition and hardship.
Thank You for the remnants. Thank You for showing
Your power by working through the few, not the many.
We trust You for the increase. Amen.

Stinkin' Thinkin'

*Let us be sober, having put on the breastplate of
faith and love, and as a helmet, the hope of salvation.*

1 Thessalonians 5:8 nasb

Women's hats aren't as popular as they once were, but you
wouldn't know it by my closet. I love accessorizing with a
perky hat to make a statement, to disguise a bad hair day, or
to keep my brain from sautéing in the sizzling Florida sun. The
Bible says we need to protect our minds from bad spiritual
rays too. Nasty input produces nasty output: stinkin' thinkin'.
When we're tempted to input a questionable movie or book,
let's don our salvation helmets and say, "No way!"

*Dear Father, forgive me for the times I have ignored the
little voice in my head that warned me I was saying, doing,
watching, or reading something sinful. Help me not be
afraid of looking weird to the world. Help me fill my
mind and heart with things that please You. Amen.*

REDEEMING PAIN

I may have fallen, but I will get up; I may be
sitting in the dark, but the LORD is my light.
MICAH 7:8 CEV

"Life *is* pain, Highness. Anyone who says differently is selling something."

This memorable line from the movie, *The Princess Bride*, rings true. Pain is inevitable in life, but God can use it for redemptive purposes. Pain can knock us down, cast us into darkness, and make us feel defeated. But it's only as debilitating as we allow it to be. We *will* get up again; we *will* learn, adapt and grow through redeeming pain.

Dear Lord, we thank You that our suffering—our pain—
produces things in us that You desire: perseverance, character,
and hope. Thank You for the redeeming pain in our lives that
makes us more and more like Your precious Son. Help us to
rejoice in our sanctification, even when it hurts. Amen.

MAID OF HONOR

For I fully expect and hope that. . .my life will
bring honor to Christ, whether I live or I die.
PHILIPPIANS 1:20 NLT

Honor. A word not as respected in our society as it once was. In these days of suggestive attire, cohabitation without marriage, and tolerance for every behavior imaginable, it's hard to remember what *honor* means. As Christians, our hope and expectation is to honor Christ with our lives—especially in the details—because we are the only reflection of Jesus some people might ever see.

Dear Father, help us to reflect the glorious image of Your
Son—not passively but actively. It is easy to smile and think
of Jesus, but we ask You to help us smile and speak of Jesus.
There is no other name by which people can be saved. Amen.

THE SAM CREED

*If we are thrown into the blazing furnace, the God we serve
is able to deliver us. . . But even if he does not, we want you
to know, Your Majesty, that we will not serve your gods.*
DANIEL 3:17–18 NIV

Shadrach, Meshach, and Abednego were Israeli boys who
had been raised to worship God before being captured and
transported as slaves to Babylon. Ordered by their new king
to worship his god or die horribly in a fiery furnace, the boys
evoked the SAM Creed, an acronym for their names: My God
is able to deliver me, but even if He chooses not to, I will still
follow Him. Through tough times, let's resolve to live by the
SAM Creed.

*Gracious Lord, there is a fork in the road at the end of
every trial that leads either to deliverance or death.
We can be delivered from the trial or delivered right to
You. We praise You for promising to walk with us either
way and ask for Your strength to carry us through. Amen.*

21

See Ya, Self

"Blessed are the poor in spirit,
for theirs is the kingdom of heaven."
MATTHEW 5:3 NASB

We don't often think of ourselves as "poor in spirit," but this passage refers to those who are not full of themselves; those who are filled instead with God's spirit. "Poor" in this context means *selfless* rather than *selfish*; those with an attitude of dependence on God. How do we become poor in spirit and revel in the hope and promise of heaven? By emptying ourselves of *self* and the pride of self-sufficiency, and refilling ourselves with Jesus.

Dear God, we praise You that You long to give us Your
Spirit until we are filled and overflowing. You are
a God who gives Yourself. We ask to be emptied
of our selfishness and pride so there is room for
You in us. In thankful expectation, amen.

LOOSE LIPS

*We all make many mistakes. For if we could
control our tongues, we would be perfect and
could also control ourselves in every other way.*
JAMES 3:2 NLT

Many of us don't let thoughts marinate long before we spew them out of our mouths. We want to honor God with our speech but seem to spend more time dousing forest fires resulting from sparks kindled by our wagging tongues (James 3:5). Don't despair! There's hope for loose lips! The Creator of self-control is happy to loan us a muzzle (Psalm 39:1) if we sincerely want to change.

*Dear Lord, our tongues are like raging fires, and we
have burned so many—both willfully and accidentally.
Forgive us. We pray that more and more the Spirit
living in us would make our words pleasing in Your
sight. Set a guard, Lord, over our lips. Amen.*

CAT-A-TUDE VERSUS DOG-A-TUDE

Lord, the LORD Almighty, may those who
hope in you not be disgraced because of me.
PSALM 69:6 NIV

Are you a hisser or a wagger?

Perhaps you have a feline attitude: It's all about *me.* I like you for what you can do for *me.* You'll have my attention only when it's convenient for me. Me, me, me.

Or maybe you have a dog mentality: It's all about *you.* I love you unconditionally just because you're you. How can I make you happy?

God is glorified by selflessness, not selfishness. Let's strive to make our Master proud.

Dear Lord, thank You for the lessons You have crafted into
the very fabric of Your creation, even humble dogs and
(not-so-humble) cats. Help us to see where we are full of
pride and selfishness and to repent. Help us to love and
serve, like Jesus, without counting the cost. Amen.

IT'LL BE ALL RiGHT

Our comfort is abundant through Christ.
2 Corinthians 1:5 nasb

As children, there's no greater comfort than running to Mommy or Daddy and hearing, "It'll be all right." As adults, when we're frightened, dismayed, or dispirited, we yearn to run to enveloping arms for the same comfort. Abba Father—Papa God—is waiting with open arms to offer us loving comfort in our times of need. If we listen closely, we'll hear His still, small voice speak to our hearts: "It'll be all right, My child."

Lord, You are the Father of compassion and the God of all comfort. Help us to feel—even as we long for actual arms—that Your everlasting arms are already holding us. Forgive us for doubting Your love and help us cling more joyfully and more desperately to You. Amen.

I AM HIS

*My health may fail, and my spirit may
grow weak, but God remains the strength
of my heart; he is mine forever.*
PSALM 73:26 NLT

My dear friend was dying of an inoperable brain tumor. Mother of three, 48-year-old Sherill could no longer walk or care for herself, yet her voice was filled with hope as she gazed unwaveringly into my eyes and quoted this verse. She added something very significant at the end that I'll hold close to my heart and draw strength from when my time comes: "He is mine forever. . .*and I am His.*"

*Father, I thank You for my friend, for her example of
unwavering faith, and for how Your Spirit filled her with
hope to the very end. I pray that when my health fails
and my spirit grows weak—and they will—I would
draw increasing strength from You. Amen.*

COMFORTING THE COMFORTLESS

He comes alongside us when we go through hard times,
and before you know it, he brings us alongside someone
else who is going through hard times so that we can be
there for that person just as God was there for us.

2 CORINTHIANS 1:4 MSG

Heartbroken and hollow after my sixth miscarriage, I struggled to find meaning in my loss. My heavenly Father's arms comforted me when I burst into tears at song lyrics or at the sight of a mother cuddling her infant in Walmart. I finally relinquished my babies to Jesus' loving embrace, confident that I'd see them again one day. Then I was able to share His comfort and hope with other women suffering miscarriages.

Lord, as hard as it is to say, thank You for my suffering.
Thank You that I know You better because of it.
Thank You for forming my character through it. Thank
You for the fruit of comfort and salvation that You
have brought to others because of it. Amen.

27

INCREASING VISIBILITY

Where then is my hope?
JOB 17:15 NIV

On hectic days when fatigue takes its toll, when we feel like cornless husks, hope disappears. When hurting people hurt people and we're in the line of fire, hope vanishes. When ideas fizzle, efforts fail; when we throw the spaghetti against the wall and nothing sticks, hope seems lost. But we must remember it's only temporary. The mountaintop isn't gone just because it's obscured by fog. Visibility will improve tomorrow and hope will rise.

Lord, help us pick the spaghetti up off the floor, rinse it well, and serve it with a smile! You are with us in these messy, sad, uncomfortable days, when we can't see a step further than where we are right now. Help us fix our eyes on the unseen and eternal—on You. Amen.

THE EYES HAVE IT

*All of you together are Christ's body,
and each of you is a part of it.*
1 CORINTHIANS 12:27 NLT

Just as our bodies are compiled of many parts, each essential for functioning as a whole, the body of Christ is made up of hands, feet, ears, hearts, and minds. We women understand this concept but tend to compare ourselves to others. If we're hands, we wish we were feet. If we're noses, we'd rather be eyes. Sometimes we feel like bunions. But God views us as equally important, none better than another. Even us toenails!

*Dear Lord, thank You for allowing me to help build the
body of Christ—the church. Give me eyes to see needs
that I can fill, hearts that I can comfort, and minds
that I can train in righteousness. Help me serve
faithfully where You have placed me. Amen.*

WAG MORE

I am not complaining about having too little.
I have learned to be satisfied with whatever I have.
PHILIPPIANS 4:11 CEV

I oozed envy as writer buddies received awards, broke sales records, and snagged lucrative contracts. What about me? Where were my accolades? It had always been enough to know I was following God's chosen path for me, but suddenly all I could do was complain. I wanted more.

Then God sent me a sign. Actually, it was a bumper sticker on a passing car: WAG MORE, BARK LESS. Message received. . . with a smile.

Lord, there will always be someone more fortunate
than I. Help me to be grateful for what You have given
me. There will always be someone less fortunate than I.
Again, help me to be grateful for what You have given
me. That is Your will for me, and it is good. Amen.

LORD OF THE DANCE

Remember your promise to me;
it is my only hope.
PSALM 119:49 NLT

The Bible contains many promises from God: He will protect us (Proverbs 1:33), comfort us (2 Corinthians 1:5), help in our times of trouble (Psalm 46:1), and encourage us (Isaiah 40:29). The word *encourage* comes from the root phrase "to inspire courage." Like an earthly father encouraging his daughter from backstage as her steps falter during her dance recital, our Papa God wants to inspire courage in us, if we only look to Him.

Dear Father, our steps will falter. We will stumble, and our faith will fail. That's just who we are as imperfect children. Thank You for promising never to leave or forsake us. Thank You for always being there, whispering encouragement and hope in our ears. We need You so. Amen.

HOLDING HANDS

When I am afraid, I will put my trust in You.
PSALM 56:3 NASB

While I cowered in a bathroom stall before my first speaking event, my queasy stomach rolled and sweat beaded on my forehead. I prayed for a way to escape. Into my head popped a childhood memory verse: "*When I am afraid, I will put my trust in You.*" My pounding heart calmed. I repeated the scripture aloud and felt my nausea subside and panic diminish. Peace flooded my soul.

When we're afraid, Papa God is right beside us holding our hand.

Dear Lord, when the waters rise, You are the lifter of our heads. When we lose our way, You whisper which way to turn. When we are afraid, You take us by the hand. Forgive us for forgetting how close You always are. Help us to depend on You more and more. Amen.

BiGGER THAN FEAR

Having hope will give you courage.
You will be protected and will rest in safety.
JOB 11:18 NLT

Tossing, turning, sleepless nights: What woman doesn't know these intimately? Our thoughts race with the "what-ifs" and fear steals our peace. How precious is God's promise that He will rescue us from nagging, faceless fear and give us courage to *just say no* to anxious thoughts that threaten to terrorize us at our most vulnerable moments. He is our hope and protector. He is bigger than fear. Anxiety flees in His presence. Rest with Him tonight.

Lord, sometimes I am afraid to go to bed. I am afraid of the
endless night, the fears that assail me, the exhaustion that
steals my joy and my hope. On those nights, help me to
continually cry out to You, relinquishing my fears and
laying them at Your feet with thanksgiving. Amen.

LiGHT MY FiRE

If God is for us, who can be against us?
ROMANS 8:31 NIV

Some days it feels as if the entire world is conspiring to make us as miserable as possible. Your spouse is crabby, the kids forget to mention the four dozen cupcakes they volunteered you for *today*, traffic jams, your boss is on the rampage, your coworkers are in nasty moods, you forgot to defrost dinner, the car overheats again. But our God is King of the Universe, and He's on our side. Girl, if that doesn't light your fire, the wood's wet.

Dear Lord, forgive me for allowing these light and momentary troubles to fill my sight and exclude You. Give me Your perspective on them. Help me turn to You continually in prayer, both for my own sinful attitude and for the people around me. You are for all of us. Amen.

ACING THE TEST

Always be ready to give an answer
when someone asks you about your hope.
1 PETER 3:15 CEV

Remember algebra tests in high school? Instant sweat and heart palpitations. You dreaded going into them unprepared; you wanted to have answers ready so you wouldn't be left with saliva drooling from your gaping mouth when questioned. The Bible says we should be prepared when someone asks about the hope within us—the hope they couldn't help but notice radiating from our souls. The answer scores an A+ for all eternity: Jesus!

God, there is salvation in no one else, for there is no
other name under heaven by which we must be saved.
Just Jesus. That's it. Forgive us for the times we've kept
silent when we could have shared the answer to the
only question on the ultimate final exam. Amen.

CHEF D'OEUVRE

Be strong and let your heart take courage,
all you who hope in the LORD.
PSALM 31:24 NASB

Identical eggs can be turned into greasy fried egg sandwiches or an exquisite soufflé. The difference is how much beating they endure.

When life seems to be beating us down, we must remember that we are a masterpiece in progress. The mixing, slicing, and dicing may feel brutal at times, but our Lord has offered us His courage and strength to endure until He is ready to unveil the *chef d'oeuvre.*

Dear Father, thank You for loving me so much that
You are willing to work tirelessly to make me more like
Your Son. Thank You for not throwing up Your hands at my
mess but instead patiently mixing, kneading, seasoning,
and applying just the right amount of heat. Amen.

DOWN WiTH FLAB

*Exercise daily in God—no spiritual flabbiness, please!
Workouts in the gymnasium are useful, but a disciplined life
in God is far more so, making you fit both today and forever.*
1 TIMOTHY 4:8–9 MSG

Do you have Dumbo flaps? You know, those fleshy wings that hang on the underside of your arms when you raise them. A stiff wind could create liftoff. They say regular workouts will tighten those puppies up. . .and significantly reduce wind shear. Just as we exercise muscles to make them strong, we keep our faith in shape by exercising it. Discipline is the way to conquer flab—physically *and* spiritually!

*Lord, I am not who I want to be. . .yet. I know You are
working in me, sending both the trials and the joys that
build my faith into something rock-solid. Give me patience
in this process and help me to recognize both where I have
grown and what faith-muscles still need work. Amen.*

SMILING IN THE DARKNESS

The hopes of the godless evaporate.

JOB 8:13 NLT

Hope isn't just an emotion; it's a perspective, a discipline, a way of life. It's a journey of choice. We must learn to override those messages of discouragement, despair, and fear that assault us in times of trouble and press toward the light. Hope is smiling in the darkness. It's confidence that faith in God's sovereignty amounts to *something*. . .something life-changing, life-saving, and eternal.

*Lord, when I am despairing and hope seems far away,
help me remember that I always have a choice: to reject
You in that moment or to reach out to You. Forgive me
for the times I just gaze hopelessly at my own navel.
Help me remember to lift my eyes to You. Amen.*

LET ME BE

"Martha. . . you are worried and upset about many
things, but few things are needed—or indeed
only one. Mary has chosen what is better."
LUKE 10:41–42 NIV

Martha zipped around cleaning, cooking, and organizing. Meanwhile, Mary sat at Jesus' feet. Many of us think like Martha. Will food magically appear on the table? Will the house clean itself? We're slaves to endless to-do lists. Our need to do overwhelms our desire to be. Constipated calendars attest that we are human *do*ings instead of human *be*ings. But Jesus taught that Mary chose best—simply to *be.* Lord, help this *do*er learn to *be.*

Dear Father, there are so many good and needful things
to do; help me choose, like Mary, what is better. Give me
the courage to simply be still and know that You are God
and that knowing You is my highest good and my most
important priority. Everything else flows from that. Amen.

SUPERGLUE FAITH

*In Him, you also, after listening to the message of truth,
the gospel of your salvation—having also believed,
you were sealed in Him with the Holy Spirit of promise.*
EPHESIANS 1:13 NASB

Remember the old commercial that depicted a construction worker dangling in mid-air, the top of his helmet bonded by superglue to a horizontal beam? Faith is like superglue. We cling to our God, our foundation, our beam. As believers, we are sealed in Christ and the bond cannot be undone. Through prayer in times of despair, our faith is strengthened and becomes waterproof, pressure-resistant, and unbreakable.

*Dear Father, we thank You that as tightly as we hold
to You, You are holding us even tighter. No one can
pluck us out of Your almighty hands. We are saved!
We are sealed! We are eternally Yours! Help us to both
rest and to rejoice in that wonderful truth. Amen.*

SMALL BUT MIGHTY

He has. . .exalted the humble.
LUKE 1:52 NLT

God delights in making small things great. He's in the business of taking scrap-heap people and turning them into treasures: Noah (the laughingstock of his city), Moses (stuttering shepherd turned national leader), David (smallest among the big and powerful), Sarah (old and childless), Mary (poor teenager), Rahab (harlot turned faith-filled ancestor of Jesus). So you and I can rejoice with hope! Let us glory in our smallness!

Lord, when we sigh over our smallness and insignificance, help us to see that even our biggest movie stars, political leaders, or cultural trendsetters are miniscule compared to You. Nothing compares to You. And thank You for allowing us to partake of Your glory in Jesus Christ. Amen.

PICK ME UP, DADDY

Rejoice in hope of the glory of God.
ROMANS 5:2 NKJV

To rejoice means to live joyfully. . .joy-fully. . .full of joy. Joy is a decision we make. A choice *not* to keep wallowing in the mud of our lives. And there will be mud—at one time or another. When spiritual rain mixes with the dirt of fallen people, mud is the inevitable result. The Creator of sparkling sunbeams, soaring eagles, and spectacular fuchsia sunsets wants to lift us out of the mud. Why don't we raise our arms to Him today?

God, when You saved us, You lifted us from the miry clay of our sin and set us firmly on the rock of our salvation. That is where we are right now, but we always forget. Remind us, restore us, renew us. We long to see ourselves as You see us. Amen.

KEEP BREATHING, SISTER!

As long as we are alive, we still have hope,
just as a live dog is better off than a dead lion.
ECCLESIASTES 9:4 CEV

Isn't this a tremendous scripture? At first glance, the ending elicits a chuckle. But consider the truth it contains: Regardless of how powerful, regal, or intimidating a lion is, when he's dead, he's *dead.* But the living—you and I—still have hope. Limitless possibilities! Hope for today and for the future. Although we may be as lowly dogs, fresh, juicy bones abound. As long as we're breathing, it's not too late!

Dear Lord, thank You that our hope in You never fails.
No matter how often we bark at strangers, snap at our
loved ones, or chew the furniture—no matter how doglike
we act—we still have hope in Your unfailing love. You
forgive and forgive and forgive. In thanksgiving, amen.

IT'S A MYSTERY

This is the day which the LORD has made;
Let us rejoice and be glad in it.
PSALM 118:24 NASB

Let's face it, girls, some mornings our rejoicing lasts only until the toothpaste drips onto our new shirt or the toast sets off the fire alarm. But the mystery of Jesus-joy is that it's not dependent on rosy circumstances. If we, after cleaning the shirt and scraping the toast, intentionally give our day to the Lord, He *will* infuse it with His joy. Things look much better through Jesus-joy contact lenses!

Lord, seeing as You see doesn't come naturally. Joy is
something the scripture says we have to put on. We have
to choose it. Forgive us for choosing other things, when Your
joy is right there, waiting to transform our days. Thank You
that it is a supernatural choice with actual results! Amen.

DWELLiNG PLACE

*Do you not know that you are a temple of
God and that the Spirit of God dwells in you?*
1 CORINTHIANS 3:16 NASB

Have you ever been awed by the beauty of a majestic cathedral with towering ceilings inlaid with gold and silver, magnificent paintings, rich carpets, and stained glass windows? Only the finest for the house of God Almighty.

Did you know God thinks of you and me as living cathedrals—dwelling places of His Spirit? How amazing to be considered worthy of such an honor! How immeasurable His love to choose us as His dwelling place!

*Dear Lord, it seems impossible that You, the God of
the universe, would choose to live in us. But then we
remember Jesus: God putting on flesh and coming to live
among sinful people. Thank You for never giving up on
making masterpieces out of us—from the inside out. Amen.*

GOiNG THE DiSTANCE

[David]. . .chose five smooth stones from the stream. . .
and, with his sling in his hand, approached the Philistine.
1 SAMUEL 17:40 NIV

That little dude David had no intention of backing down from
his fight until it was finished. Notice he picked up *five* rocks,
not just one. He was prepared to go the distance against his
giant. He fully expected God to make him victorious, but he
knew it wouldn't be easy.

So you've used your first rock against your giant. Maybe
even your second. But don't give up. Keep reloading your
sling and go the distance. Victory is sweet!

Dear Lord, please help me to keep going the distance
even when I fail or stumble along the way. Give me
strength, courage, and hope to reload and take aim
at our foes one more time. No matter what happens,
I trust You, my warrior King, my Savior, and guide. Amen.

TOP OFF MY TANK

*"My grace is sufficient for you, for my
power is made perfect in weakness."*
2 CORINTHIANS 12:9 NIV

There is no weaker vessel than a bedraggled mother at 6 a.m.,
staring into a bathroom mirror after another rough night.
She's trying to decide if the dark smudges beneath her eyes
are yesterday's grape jelly when she suddenly realizes she's
brushing her hair with her toothbrush. Yep, we are a sisterhood
of slightly sagging spiritual warriors, but we can depend on
God to power our weak vessels. And He is able.

*Father, Your grace is greater than our grungiest T-shirts,
greater than our worst hair day, greater than our grouchiest
mornings. We praise You because You don't even notice those
things. Help us dress ourselves in the love, joy, peace, patience,
and kindness that only Your Spirit can provide. Amen.*

ENDURING WITH GRACE

*Endurance builds character, which gives
us a hope that will never disappoint us.*
ROMANS 5:4–5 CEV

Heroes come in all packages. My eighteen-year-old niece, Andie, has cerebral palsy and is legally blind. It takes her four times longer than the average person to do just about anything. But she does it anyway: playing drums, walking in leg braces, attending college. Some days, the frustration of being *different* overwhelms her. But through endurance, she has developed inspiring character traits—rock-solid faith, contagious hope, and a stellar sense of humor. When I grow up, I want to be like Andie.

*Dear Lord, thank You for Andie's example of how suffering
can produce character. I want to be like that too, Lord,
even in my small struggles. I pray You would give me eyes
to see how You are working through the hard things
in my life and faith to continue trusting. Amen.*

HEAVYWEIGHT

This hope is like a firm and
steady anchor for our souls.
HEBREWS 6:19 CEV

Julia and Mark anchored their sailboat to do a little reef exploring while they went diving. When they surfaced, the boat was a speck on the horizon. It had drifted more than a half-mile because their anchor wasn't heavy enough to withstand the strong current.

Hope in Christ is an anchor for our souls. But if the anchor isn't sturdy—weighted by firm and steady faith—we may drift in strong currents of doubt, problems, and disillusionment. Weigh your anchor today.

Lord, I know You have kept me from smashing into jagged
rocks many times. I've drifted, and You've protected me.
Remind me daily—hourly—to pray and to dive deep into
Your Word, so that my anchor will not drag but stay
firmly lodged in the Rock of my Salvation. Amen.

BRICK BY BRICK

So then faith cometh by hearing,
and hearing by the word of God.
ROMANS 10:17 KJV

Words are powerful. They cut. They heal. They confirm. God uses His Word to help us, to mold us, to make us more like Him. Our faith is built from the bricks of God's Word. Brick by brick, we erect, strengthen, and fortify that faith. But only if we truly listen and *hear* the Word of God.

Father, we can listen to Your Word for years without
truly hearing it. Only Your Spirit can enliven it and us
so that it becomes the living Word. We pray that our
hearts would be softened to the message in Your Word
and that our wills would be conformed to it. Amen.

A PERFECT FIT

The LORD is good to those whose hope
is in him, to the one who seeks him.
LAMENTATIONS 3:25 NIV

Seeking God is, for some, like a child groping in a dark room for the light switch. She knows it's there, she just can't seem to put her fingers on it. Some search for God all their lives, trying on various religions like pairs of shoes. This one pinches. That one chafes. But we must bypass religious fluff for the heart of the matter: Jesus. The only way to God is through faith in Christ (John 14:6). Suddenly, the shoe fits!

Dear Father, thank You that I found You—or, rather,
that You found me. Suddenly, the crazy world makes
sense; the light switch has been flipped on, and I can
finally see. I praise You for my salvation! And I praise
You for being the light of the whole world. Amen.

ROOTS

"There is hope for your future," declares the LORD,
"And your children will return to their own territory."
JEREMIAH 31:17 NASB

Prodigal. The word alone evokes an involuntary shudder.

Most of us know parents whose children have left home in the throes of rebellion. Some of us *are* those parents. After years of protecting and nurturing our children, heartache replaces harmony, panic supersedes pride. Broken relationships shred our hearts with their jagged edges. But the Great Peacemaker declares that prodigals will one day return to their roots. One of His greatest parables reinforces that hope (Luke 15).

Dear Father, we were all prodigal children until we accepted the once-for-all sacrifice of Your Son. We praise You that You are not willing that any should perish, but that all come to a saving knowledge of Jesus Christ. And we will continue to pray, in faith, until that day comes. Amen.

LEGACY OF LOVE

After all, when the Lord Jesus appears,
who else but you will give us hope and joy
and be like a glorious crown for us?
1 Thessalonians 2:19 cev

The most hope-inspiring legacy we can pass on to the next generation is faith. What delight it is for us as women to plant and nurture seeds of faith in our children, knowing that at harvest they'll stand by our sides before the Lord Jesus! It's never too late to till the fertile soil of their hearts by our example of daily Bible reading, prayer, and dependence on our Savior.

Lord, forgive my busy, self-focused life, my lack of prayer,
my neglect of Your Word. Please help me be an example
for my children of a life lived in joy and dependence on
You. I pray that Your strength would be made perfect
in my weakness, even in this. Amen.

I'VE GOT A NAME

*"I have redeemed you; I have called
you by your name; you are Mine."*
ISAIAH 43:1 NKJV

Parents have the indescribable privilege of bestowing a name on their newborn. The identity that little person will be known by for the rest of his or her life. In effect, we give them a part of us. They are an extension of ourselves—our flesh, our blood.

Your heavenly Father has called you by name. He has given you part of Himself: Jesus. You are special to Him. You are His daughter. In this, find security. . .comfort. . .hope.

*Dear Heavenly Father, thank You for calling me by name,
out of the darkness and into the light. Thank You for
being my Abba, my Daddy. I long for the day when I
will run to Your outstretched arms and hear You say,
"Well done." Until then, Lord, I trust in You. Amen.*

Jets and Submarines

No power in the sky above or in the earth below—indeed,
nothing in all creation will ever be able to separate us from
the love of God that is revealed in Christ Jesus our Lord.
Romans 8:39 NLT

Have you ever been diving amid the spectacular array of vivid color and teeming life in the silent world under the sea? Painted fish of rainbow hues are backlit by diffused sunbeams. Multi-textured coral dot the gleaming white sand. You honestly feel as if you're in another world. But every world is God's world. He soars above the clouds with us and spans the depths of the seas. *Nothing* can separate us from His love.

Dear Lord, I praise You because Your love is so strong
that nothing can separate me from it. No sin that I
commit, no terrible thought, nothing done to me by
someone else. Your love is greater, stronger, deeper,
wider, and longer than anything in all creation. Amen.

HiS LiTTLE GiRLS

Just as a father has compassion on his children,
so the LORD has compassion on those who fear Him.
PSALM 103:13 NASB

Plagued with horrible recurring nightmares during my childhood, I remember the terror of waking up screaming, hair sweat-plastered to my face. Then like a candle in the darkness, my father would appear at my bedside, lie beside me, and gently rub my back until I fell asleep. Our heavenly Father is like that—tender, caring, protective. And He too responds when His little girls need comfort from His loving presence.

Dear God, thank You for the earthly father who comforted
me so well and showed me a glimpse, early on, of what
Your love is like. I offer my grown-up fears to You, Lord—
my fears of death, disease, disaster, loneliness. Please
comfort me; be with me in the night. Amen.

HiS HEART'S DELiGHT

The LORD's delight is in those who fear him,
those who put their hope in his unfailing love.
PSALM 147:11 NLT

Do you remember how you felt when you witnessed a baby's first faltering steps? *Delight.* That's what it was. Just like when you heard her sing "Jesus Loves Me" in her squeaky, off-key voice, or she served you tea in tiny pink teacups. The Bible says the Lord delights in us, His children, the very same way. We warm His heart and bring a smile to His lips when we honor Him with our lives. He *delights* in us.

Lord, You created my inmost being; You knit me together
in my mother's body. I am fearfully and wonderfully
made. Forgive me for losing sight of that in the bustle
of life. I pray You would graciously show me just a
glimpse today of how You delight in me. Amen.

REST STOP

So let's not allow ourselves to get fatigued
doing good. At the right time we will harvest
good crop if we don't give up, or quit.
GALATIANS 6:9 MSG

As women, we're used to serving others. It's part of the feminine package. But sometimes we get burned out. Fatigued. Overburdened. Girls, God doesn't want us to be washed-out dishrags, to be so boggled that we try to pay for groceries with our library card. It's up to us to recognize the symptoms and rest, regroup, reenergize. This is not indulgent; it's *necessary* to do our best in His name. So give yourself permission to rest. Today.

Father, thank You for the reminder that rest is good.
You know we are part of a body, and the body won't
function as well if even a tiny part is injured, exhausted,
or just fed up with life. Help us learn to recognize when we,
like Jesus, need to regroup and recharge. Amen.

LET THE SUN SHINE IN

*"Come to me, all you who are weary
and burdened, and I will give you rest."*
MATTHEW 11:28 NIV

Nothing chokes hope like weariness. Day in and day out drudgery produces weariness of body, heart, and soul. It feels like dark clouds have obscured the sun and cast us into perpetual shadow. But Jesus promised rest for our weary souls, respite from our burdens and healing for our wounds. . .*if* we come to Him. The sun isn't really gone, it's just hidden until the clouds roll away.

Dear Lord, I want to know what it really means to come to You. I don't want to make You just another item on my to-do list, to be squeezed in between grocery shopping and carpooling. I want to orient my life around You. You promise rest. . .if I come. Amen.

No Wimps Here

For God has not given us a spirit of fear and
timidity, but of power, love, and self-discipline.
2 Timothy 1:7 nlt

Do you suffer paralysis by analysis? Are you so afraid of trying
something new that you put it off until you can think it through
. . .and end up doing nothing at all? Too much introspection
creates inertia, and we abhor the ineffective wimps we become.
Sisters, God never intended for us to be wimps. His power and
love are available to replace our fear and infuse us with courage.
Shake off that paralysis and get moving!

God, I praise You for being a God of action: for creating,
redeeming, fighting, rescuing, planning, moving, saving.
You are always working for our good. Forgive me for being
paralyzed by my own thinking sometimes. Help me to draw
closer to You and partake of Your active power. Amen.

BATTLE PLAN

I sought the LORD, and He answered me,
and delivered me from all my fears.
PSALM 34:4 NASB

There is nothing more wasteful than fear. Fear paralyzes, destroys potential, and shatters hope. It's like an enemy attacking from our blind side. But we don't have to allow fear to defeat us. It's a war that we can win! First comes earnest prayer, then comes change. God will deliver us from our fears if we seek Him and follow His battle plan.

Dear Lord, over and over in Your Word, You say, "Do not fear." Thank You for never giving us commands that You don't also give us the means to obey. Help me to hate my fears instead of using them as excuses. Help me to seek You. . .and expect You to answer. Amen.

THEY'RE JUST MEN

*"He may have a great army, but they are
merely men. We have the LORD our God
to help us and to fight our battles for us!"*
2 CHRONICLES 32:8 NLT

When facing attack from an enemy army, Hezekiah uttered these profound words: "They're *just* men. The God of All Creation is standing by to fight for us! No comparison!" And sure enough, against all human reasoning, God sent an angel to defeat the entire enemy army (2 Chronicles 32:21). God still intervenes today to help us fight our battles, whether supernaturally or by natural means. Trust Him. He's got His armor on.

*Dear God, so often I try to fight battles in my own strength
and wonder why my plans fail. I never consult You or other
wise counselors; I don't look for wisdom in Your Word.
Forgive me for my pride and independence. They are
illusions; my strength is only in You. Amen.*

GO FOR IT

When everything was hopeless, Abraham believed
anyway, deciding to live not on the basis of what he
saw he couldn't do but on what God said he would do.
ROMANS 4:18 MSG

"You can't do that. It's impossible." Have you ever been told this?
Or just thought it because of fear or a previous experience
with failure?

This world is full of those who discourage rather than
encourage. If we believe them, we'll never do anything. But if
we, like Abraham, believe that God has called us for a particular
purpose, we'll go for it despite our track records. Past failure
doesn't dictate future failure. If God wills it, He fulfills it.

Dear Lord, You are the God of the impossible. We praise
You when we remember how many times You have rescued,
healed, and intervened in impossible ways for Your people.
Help us to live hopefully in the light of Your promises,
knowing nothing is impossible for You. Amen.

WHEN I'M BA-A-AD

*"I am the good shepherd; I know my
own sheep, and they know me, just as my
Father knows me and I know the Father."*
JOHN 10:14–15 NLT

Ever spent much time around sheep? They're really self-centered. All they think about is eating, sleeping, and avoiding conflict. A lot like me. But one good thing about sheep is that they'll drop everything and respond to their shepherd's voice. Not anybody else's voice, just the familiar tones of their own shepherd they've learned to trust and follow. This little ewe wants to recognize and respond to her beloved Shepherd's voice too. How about you, ewe?

*Dear Father, sometimes it irks me that I am a sheep.
I want to be something more important, maybe higher
up on the food chain! Forgive me for chafing against
how You've made me and help me to listen and respond
to Your loving voice when You speak. Amen.*

NOTHING MORE THAN FEELINGS

*LORD, sustain me as you promised, that I
may live! Do not let my hope be crushed.*
PSALM 119:116 NLT

Whatever our foe—unemployment, rejection, loss, illness—we may feel beaten down by life. Hope feels crushed by the relentless boulder bearing down on our souls. We feel that we can't possibly endure another day. Yes, we feel, we *feel.* But feelings are often deceiving. God promises to sustain us, to strengthen us, so that we might withstand that massive rock. We can trust Him. He will not allow us to be crushed!

*Lord, we are lost, crushed, abandoned, alone. It's all too
hard, and You feel so far away. Sustain us, dear Father,
in this hardship. Only You can keep our hope alive and
the flame of our faith from going out. We trust You
and cling to You in this darkness. Amen.*

TRUMPED

*And the L*ORD *said to Abraham, "Why did Sarah laugh, saying, 'Shall I indeed bear a child, when I am so old?' Is anything too difficult for the L*ORD*?"*
GENESIS 18:13–14 NASB

Sarah, well past menopause and losing the drooping appendage war, was so floored when told of her impending pregnancy that she burst into laughter. How absurd to think those breasts sagging to her navel would nurse a baby! But that's exactly what God had in store. We sometimes forget that God *created* the systems we consider absolute and impenetrable. He can trump them all with a flick of His pinkie!

Dear God, we praise You for doing the impossible for Sarah and take comfort in the unshakeable fact that You can do the same for us. There is no prayer too wild for You. Thank You that we are never too old and useless to see Your hand at work in our lives. Amen.

TOLERANCE ISN'T ENOUGH

"In his name the nations will put their hope."
MATTHEW 12:21 NIV

In the summer of 2000, my husband and I toured the Holy Land. Our Israeli guide assured us that there was no safer place than Jerusalem, for people of numerous faiths—Muslim, Jewish, Christian, Hindu—had learned tolerance as the key to living together peaceably. Yet tension was as evident as the armed guards on every street corner. Violence erupted three months later with the first bus bombings. Our only hope for peace is Jehovah.

Lord, so often we think that a perfect world is actually something we can achieve. We look to leaders and laws and localities, forgetting that we are all fallen creatures on a fallen world, waiting—longing—for the day when You will make all things new. Come, Lord Jesus. Amen.

REDEEMED!

*O Israel, hope in the LORD; for with the LORD there is
lovingkindness, and with Him is abundant redemption.*
PSALM 130:7 NASB

The Psalmist knew Israel had a rotten track record. Throughout
Old Testament history, God miraculously delivered the Israelites
from trouble repeatedly, and they would gratefully turn to Him,
only to eventually slip again into rebellion and more trouble.
Sounds a lot like you and me, doesn't it? But thankfully, ours is
a redemptive God; a God who offers abundant lovingkindness
and forgiveness. A God of second chances—then and now.

*Dear God, we look at Israel and think, How could they?
How could they have seen the miracles and continued in
rebellion and forgetfulness? Forgive us, Lord, for thinking
we are any different. Forgive us our wickedness, rebellion,
and sin. Thank You for Your endless, loving faithfulness. Amen.*

MR. CLEAN FOR THE SOUL

*As far as the east is from the west, so far has
He removed our transgressions from us.*
PSALM 103:12 NASB

Dirty little secrets. We all have them. Exposing them is a popular theme for television shows these days. But we don't have to wallow in the muck of our past. God has promised to wash us clean of our dirty little secrets and remove them as far as the east is from the west when we repent of our wrongdoings and ask him for forgiveness. An immaculate and sparkling fresh start—redemption is Mr. Clean for the soul!

*Father, we praise You for Jesus' example of sinlessness in
thought, deed, and word. That is a standard of perfection
that we can never meet, but because He took our sins as
His own, we can rest in His righteousness. Thank You
for paying the price we could not. Amen.*

QUESTiONS AND ANSWERS

And the Scriptures were written to teach
and encourage us by giving us hope.
ROMANS 15:4 CEV

What do you do when facing a perplexing problem? Ask a family member? Consult a friend? Turn to the internet?

God's Word is brimming with answers to life's difficulties, yet it's often the last place we turn. God speaks to us today through the lives of trusting Abraham, broken-hearted Ruth, runaway Jonah, courageous Esther, female leader Deborah in a male-dominated society, beaten-down Job, double-crossing Peter, and Paul, who proved people *can* change.

Dear Lord, You hold all the answers to every question that has
ever been asked—or ever will be asked. Nothing surprises,
shocks, or confounds You. Thank You for being the Alpha
and Omega, the beginning and the end. Help me to look
to You—and into Your Word—for answers. Amen.

HIT THE MATS

Blessed are those whose help is the God of Jacob,
whose hope is in the LORD their God.
PSALM 146:5 NIV

Wrestled with God lately?

We all do at one time or another. The Genesis 32 account of Jacob's Almighty wrestling match reassures us that God is not offended when we beat on His chest and shout, "Why?" He understands that we must sometimes wrestle out the mysteries of our faith. Wrestling with his Lord was a turning point for Jacob—he got a new name (Israel) and a new perspective. God is ready to do the same for us.

We praise You, Lord, that You are strong and loving
enough to take our feeble blows. When our faith falters
and we want to blame You and wrestle through our
doubts and questions, You do not waver. Please turn our
fears to faith and our doubts to knowledge. Amen.

GiRLFRiENDS

*And our hope for you is firm, because
we know that just as you share in our
sufferings, so also you share in our comfort.*

2 CORINTHIANS 1:7 NIV

Anne of Green Gables was right: Bosom friends are important. Girls need girlfriends. . .little girls and grown-up girls alike. God wired us to need each other, to yearn for the heart-bonding that results from sharing sufferings, comfort, hugs, and giggles. Nothing's wrong with men, of course, but they don't make the same bosom friends as girls. Have you thanked the Lord lately for your soul-sisters?

*Dear Father, thank You so much for giving me sisters in Christ.
Thank You for the friends who offer quiet encouragement,
for those who challenge my faith, for those who push me to
try new things, for those who offer practical help. They
are immeasurably precious gifts from You. Amen.*

ONE FOR ALL

*All of you are part of the same body. There is only
one Spirit of God, just as you were given one hope
when you were chosen to be God's people.*

EPHESIANS 4:4 CEV

Remember the motto of the Three Musketeers? "All for one
and one for all." Christ-followers should have the same sense
of unity, for we are bound together by eternal hope, the gift of
our Savior. Feeling *with* and *for* each other, we'll cry tears of
joy from one eye and tears of sadness from the other. Loneliness is not an option. Take the first step. Reach out today—
someone else's hand is reaching too.

*Lord, sometimes we are afraid to reach out. We are afraid
of being needy, a nuisance, or of being rejected. Forgive us
for not trusting Your Body. Help us to see those hands
reaching out to us as Your hands and to clasp them
without fear. In Jesus' Name, amen.*

BFF

I am counting on the LORD; yes, I am counting on him. I have put my hope in his word.
PSALM 130:5 NLT

"Best Friends Forever" earn this title of honor because we've learned we can count on them. They've proven they'll be there for us through svelte and bloated, sweet and grumpy, thoughtful and insensitive. Bailing us out of countless sinking dinghies, they've held us as we sobbed, fed our families, watched our kids, and made us smile. How much more can we count on our Creator to be there for us?

Dear Father, we praise You that You have hands and feet on this earth, and they are the body of Christ. Forgive us for how our words and actions or lack of actions have hurt it. Help us to use our gifts to build up our local body—our church. Amen.

HEAVEN'S BAKERY

*"Those who hope in me
will not be disappointed."*
ISAIAH 49:23 NIV

As I stood in line ogling luscious pastries in the coffee shop's glass case, I asked the teenage clerk which she would suggest. Casting cornflower-blue eyes heavenward, she tapped her dainty chin with one finger before answering in a wistful voice. "I recommend the blueberry cheesecake. When I eat it, I hear angels." What higher recommendation is there? What greater hope have we than heaven? (Maybe they'll even serve blueberry cheesecake there!)

Lord, that cheesecake was delicious, and each bite made me think of heaven. But heaven is going to be so much more. Thank You for that little taste of glory. Thank You for the pleasures You give in this life. . .and the pleasure I will taste at Your right hand, forever. Amen.

HEADING HOME

*We are only foreigners living
here on earth for a while.*
1 CHRONICLES 29:15 CEV

I quivered on the icy Alps peak, more from fear than cold. Which ski slope was my level (beginner) and which were treacherously advanced? A mistake could be deadly. Panic gripped me; I couldn't read the German signs and no one spoke English.

As Christians, we're foreigners on this earth. We don't speak the same language or share the same perspective as nonbelievers. We're only passing through this world on our way to the next. . .heading home.

*Lord, thank You for getting me down that mountain in one
piece. Thank You for the many times You have protected
me and gotten me out of jams of my own making. I ask for
continued protection and guidance as I try to navigate
this foreign world and make my way home. Amen.*

BEYOND THE HORIZON

Always continue to fear the Lord. You will be rewarded
for this; your hope will not be disappointed.
Proverbs 23:17–18 nlt

Have you ever traversed a long, winding road, unable to see your final destination? Perhaps you were surprised by twists and turns along the way or jarred by unexpected potholes. But you were confident that if you stayed on *that* road, you would eventually reach your destination. Likewise, God has mapped out our futures. The end of the road may disappear beyond the horizon, but we are assured that our destination will not be disappointing.

Dear Lord, You see the end from the beginning, and nothing
surprises You. Thank You for the confidence that gives us
when we trust in You. When we can't see how the next
hour is going to turn out—even less the next day—
we hope in You. In grateful trust, amen.

NEVER ALONE

I am convinced that nothing can ever separate us from God's love. Neither death nor life, neither angels nor demons, neither our fears for today nor our worries about tomorrow—not even the powers of hell can separate us from God's love.

ROMANS 8:38 NLT

I read a poll that said being alone is one of women's worst fears. When we experience loss, we sometimes feel that we're struggling all alone; that others around us can't possibly comprehend the scope of our fears, our worries, our pain. But the Bible says we're not alone, that *nothing* can separate us from our heavenly Father. He is right there beside us, loving us, offering His companionship when we have none.

Dear Father, it is hard for me to feel Your presence sometimes, but I trust Your Word. It says I am not alone; it says Your Spirit is with me; it says Jesus is always interceding for me. Forgive me for doubting and help me to walk by faith, not by sight. Amen.

I DO

Let us hold unswervingly to the hope we
profess, for he who promised is faithful.
HEBREWS 10:23 NIV

An important part of any marriage is the vow of faithfulness. We pledge that we will remain faithful to our beloved until death do us part. Faithfulness is *crucial* to a trusting relationship. We must be able to depend on our spouse to always be in our corner, love us even when we're unlovable, and never leave or forsake us.

God is faithful. We can unswervingly depend on Him to never break His promises.

Lord, so many of us have been betrayed by unfaithful
friends, family members, or spouses. And we too have
been unfaithful to others. Forgive us. You are the only
One who will never leave us or betray us or forget us,
even for a moment. We cling to You. Amen.

CAN YOU HEAR ME NOW?

But as for me, I watch in hope for the LORD,
I wait for God my Savior; my God will hear me.
MICAH 7:7 NIV

If there's anything more frustrating than waiting for someone who never shows, it's trying to talk to someone who isn't listening. It's as if they have plugged their ears and nothing penetrates. Mothers are well acquainted with this exercise in futility, as are wives, daughters, and sisters. But the Bible tells us that God hears us when we talk to Him. He shows up when we wait for Him. He will not disappoint us.

Dear God, we are thankful for Your Spirit which both
shows us our sin and gives us the strength to change.
Help us never to be guilty of ignoring Your voice—
or the voices of those around us. Give us ears to listen,
knowing You are the God who hears. Amen.

A New Tomorrow

*Rahab the harlot. . .Joshua spared. . .for she hid
the messengers whom Joshua sent to spy out Jericho.*
JOSHUA 6:25 NASB

Rahab was the unlikeliest of heroes: a prostitute who sold her body in the darkest shadows. Yet she was the very person God chose to fulfill His prophecy. How astoundingly freeing! Especially for those of us ashamed of our past or who feel we've strayed too far from God to ever be used by Him. God loved Rahab for who she was—not what she did. Rahab is proof that God can and will use anyone for His higher purposes. *Anyone.* Even you and me.

> *Lord, You have formed me in an ordinary sort of way,
> without x-ray vision or the ability to fly. But I can do
> Your will, because You have given me Your strength.
> And that is more than enough. Thank You for being
> willing to use me—a sinner—just like Rahab. Amen.*

PURE AND UNSPOILED

And everyone who has this hope fixed on
Him purifies himself, just as He is pure.
1 JOHN 3:3 NASB

Don't you just love taking the first scoop of ice cream from a fresh half-gallon? There's something about the smooth surface of unspoiled purity that satisfies the soul. It's the same with new jars of peanut butter, freshly fallen snow, or stretches of pristine, early morning beach sand. God looks at us that way—unblemished, pure and unspoiled—through our faith and hope in Him. Allow that thought to bring a smile to your face today.

Dear Father, while we were yet sinners, Christ
died for us. Thank You for that great gift of imputed
righteousness, so that we too can be washed clean
and white as snow. Help us to live with that hope fixed
unwaveringly in our hearts. We love You. Amen.

UNFATHOMABLE GRACE

Jesus treated us much better than we deserve. He made us acceptable to God and gave us the hope of eternal life.
TITUS 3:7 CEV

Whereas justice is getting what we deserve and mercy is *not* getting what we deserve, grace is getting what we *don't* deserve. Thankfully, God doesn't automatically dole out justice for our myriad sins, but reaches beyond to mercy and even a step further to grace. As Jean Valjean discovers in the classic story, *Les Miserables,* when we truly grasp God's unfathomable mercy and grace, we are then empowered to extend it to others.

Dear Father, thank You for the depth of Your mercy. You have saved me from what I deserve, and, just like Jean Valjean, I have a new name. I am not who I once was. Forgive me for taking grace lightly and not wanting to share it with everyone I meet. Amen.

THE PALM OF HIS HAND

*If I ride the wings of the morning, if I dwell by
the farthest oceans, even there your hand will
guide me, and your strength will support me.*

PSALM 139:9–10 NLT

Surf foamed around my ankles as I lifted the burgundy star-fish, its pointed tips curled in taut contraction. "It's okay little fellow, I'll help you," I crooned, gently cradling the sea creature stranded by the outgoing tide. Tiny tentacles tickled my palm as the starfish relaxed, safe and protected. Likewise, God's hand rescues, supports, and guides us to life-sustaining waters when we're stranded. We're safe in the palm of His hand.

*Dear Father, thank You for holding me so gently and
carefully in the palm of Your mighty hand. Thank You for
Your wings, spread over me against the storms. I don't
need to worry; I can relax and uncurl and breathe,
knowing You are always there. Amen.*

ROLL DOWN THE WINDOW

"Ask and it will be given to you; seek and you will find; knock and the door will be opened to you."
<small>LUKE 11:9 NIV</small>

Does your fellow have trouble asking directions? Do you cruise about the country on a scenic tour that could have been avoided by asking a simple question? We all find it difficult to some degree when it comes to asking for help. But that's how we reach our final destinations—and not just on the highway. God offers help if we only ask. He's standing there holding the road map. We just have to stop and roll down the window.

Dear God, we are asking for help today. We don't know which way to turn; we don't know the lay of the land or even which way is up. But we trust You. You have never steered us wrong. We seek Your direction. Speak to us, Lord, in our time of need. Amen.

CHERISHED DESIRE

*God our Father loves us. He is kind and has given
us eternal comfort and a wonderful hope.*

2 Thessalonians 2:16 cev

Webster's definition of *hope*: "to cherish a desire with expectation." In other words, yearning for something wonderful
you *expect* to occur. Our hope in Christ is not just yearning for
something wonderful, as in "I hope for a sunny beach day." It's
a deep trust with roots that extend from the beginning of time
to the infinite future. Our hope is not just the anticipation of
heaven, but the expectation of a fulfilling life walking beside
our Creator and best Friend.

*Lord, I am saved both now and in the future. That is a mystery
too great for me. I praise You because You are too great for
me, yet You love me so much You would die for me. That love
is mine now and forever. In Jesus' precious Name, amen.*

SEEKING AN OASIS

He changes a wilderness into a pool of water
and a dry land into springs of water.
PSALM 107:35 NASB

The wilderness of Israel is truly a barren wasteland—nothing but rocks and parched sand stretching as far as the distant horizon. The life-and-death contrast between stark desert and pools of oasis water is startling.

Our lives can feel parched too. Colorless. Devoid of life. But God has the power to transform desert lives into gurgling, spring-of-water lives. Ask Him to bubble up springs of hope within you today.

Dear Lord, You know how I am feeling today. Something I
longed for has been taken away, and even though the
trees outside are bright with autumn color, I am dull and
gray inside. Please come in, Lord. Please revive my
hope and my spirit as only You can. Amen.

NAME ABOVE ALL NAMES

*O God, we give glory to you all day long
and constantly praise your name.*
PSALM 44:8 NLT

So what has God done that deserves our everlasting praise? His descriptive names tell the story: A friend that sticks closer than a brother (Proverbs 18:24), Altogether lovely (Song of Solomon 5:16), The rock that is higher than I (Psalm 61:2), My strength and my song (Isaiah 12:2), The lifter of my head (Psalm 3:3), Shade from the heat (Isaiah 25:4). His very name fills us with hope!

God, there are not enough words in all the languages on earth to praise You adequately. Nothing we can say or sing or shout would ever express just who You are or what You have done for us. Father, Savior, Counselor—You are worthy of all our praises, now and eternally. Amen.

FiRST LOVE

*But you must stay deeply rooted and firm
in your faith. You must not give up the hope
you received when you heard the good news.*
Colossians 1:23 cev

Do you remember the day you turned your life over to Christ? Can you recall the flood of joy and hope that coursed through your veins? Ah, the wonder of first love. Like romantic love that deepens and broadens with passing years, our relationship with Jesus evolves into a river of faith that endures the test of time.

Dear Lord, we praise You for faith, which is not something we could conjure up ourselves; it is a gift of Your Spirit. We praise You that faith is strong enough to live on. It is our present help and our future hope. Help us cling to it, for better or worse. Amen.

FEEL THE LOVE

Long before he laid down earth's foundations,
he had us in mind, had settled on us as the focus
of his love, to be made whole and holy by his love.
EPHESIANS 1:4 MSG

Need a boost of hope today? Read this passage aloud, inserting your name for each "us." Wow! Doesn't that bring home the message of God's incredible, extravagant, customized love for you? I am the *focus* of His love, and I bask in the hope of healing, wholeness, and holiness His individualized attention brings. You too, dear sister, are His focus. Allow yourself to feel the love today.

Dear Father, long before You laid down earth's
foundations, You had me in mind, had settled on me
as the focus of Your love, to be made whole and holy
by Your love. I stand amazed at this love. All I can say
is thank You, thank You. In grateful praise, amen.

FOREVER AND ALWAYS

*"Never will I leave you;
never will I forsake you."*
HEBREWS 13:5 NIV

Unconditional love. We all yearn for it—from our parents, our spouses, our children, our friends. Love *not* based on our performance or accomplishments, but on who we are deep down beneath the fluff. God promises unconditional love to those who honor Him. We don't need to worry about disappointing Him when He gets to know us better—He knows us already. Better than we know ourselves. And He loves us anyway, forever and always.

*God, You are the only One who actually loves
us unconditionally—with no strings attached,
no clauses or codicils. We can do nothing to earn
Your love, and You promise never to take that love
away. Help us to love others the way You love us. Amen.*

ASTOUNDING RESCUE

*Then I remember something that fills me with
hope. The LORD's kindness never fails! If he had
not been merciful, we would have been destroyed.*
LAMENTATIONS 3:21–22 CEV

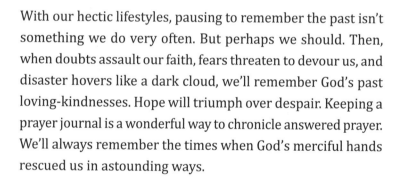

With our hectic lifestyles, pausing to remember the past isn't
something we do very often. But perhaps we should. Then,
when doubts assault our faith, fears threaten to devour us, and
disaster hovers like a dark cloud, we'll remember God's past
loving-kindnesses. Hope will triumph over despair. Keeping a
prayer journal is a wonderful way to chronicle answered prayer.
We'll always remember the times when God's merciful hands
rescued us in astounding ways.

*Dear Lord, help me pause and remember and speak
of Your faithfulness. Let me mark these instances in my
journal, just as the Israelites did when they left piles of
stones as reminders to themselves and their children.
Teach me to look back in thankfulness. Amen.*

KEEPiNG US iN STiTCHES

The secret things belong to the LORD our God.
DEUTERONOMY 29:29 NIV

Have you ever noticed the messy underside of a needlepoint picture? Ugly knots, loose threads, and clashing colors appear random, without pattern. Yet if you turn it over, an exquisite intricate design is revealed, each stitch blending to create a beautiful finished picture. Such is the fabric of our lives. The knots and loose threads may not make sense to us, but the Master Designer has a plan. The secret design *belongs* to Him.

Lord, sometimes the only way we can continue putting one foot in front of the other when doubts and disasters assail us is because we know that You are in control. You have a purpose and a plan, and someday we will stand in awe of the design You have created. Amen.

LARGE AND IN CHARGE

"In this world you will have trouble.
But take heart! I have overcome the world."
JOHN 16:33 NIV

"Who's in charge here?" Most mothers have had the experience of returning home to a chaos-wrecked house. Toys, books, clothes, snack wrappers everywhere. "Why isn't [insert correct answer here: your father, the babysitter, Grandma, etc.] in control?"

Our world can sometimes feel chaotic like that. Things appear to be spinning out of control. But we must remember that God is large and in charge. He has a plan.

Dear Lord, just like a young child does not understand the schedules, rules, and habits of his parents and how they contribute to a peaceful household, so we do not understand Your workings in this world. Why trouble, Lord? But we take heart because You have already overcome. Amen.

ONE HUNKY VERSE

To Him who is able to do far more abundantly beyond
all that we ask or think, according to the power that works
within us, to Him be the glory. . .forever and ever. Amen.
Ephesians 3:20–21 nasb

Don't you just love the *bigness* of this verse? It radiates with the enormity of God—that *nothing* is beyond His scope or power. Read it aloud and savor the words *far more abundantly*. Now repeat "beyond *all* that we ask or think" three times, pondering each word individually. Wow! If there was ever a hunky verse to cast an attitude of gratitude over our day, this is it. Yay God!

Father, when I read this verse, I wonder why I worry!
Your power is immense, and it is at work in me! You
can do anything. I'll say it again—You can do anything.
In prayer, I place my worries into the path of that
power. . .and watch and see what happens. Amen.

ONLY THE BEST

I have hidden your word in my heart
that I might not sin against you.

PSALM 119:11 NLT

I adore homemade chicken salad. Honey mustard, sliced grapes, and slivered almonds make it delicious. Quality ingredients produce quality results. But you can't make good chicken salad if all you have to work with are gizzards. It's all poultry, but there's a big difference between white meat and gizzards.

Memorizing scripture is like preparing chicken salad for the soul. God's Word (quality ingredients) will be ready at a moment's notice to guide, comfort, and train us in righteousness (quality results).

Anything else is just gizzards.

Dear Lord, I pray Your Spirit would guide me in wisdom
and discernment. Help me put no unclean thing before
my eyes and ears or into my heart and mind. Help me,
instead, fill my mind and heart with Your Word
so that it dwells in me richly. Amen.

A LifETiME AWARD

O Lord, you alone are my hope.
I've trusted you, O LORD, from childhood.
PSALM 71:5 NLT

My heart swelled like an over-inflated balloon. Tears blurred my vision as little Josh bounded for the stage, his blond cowlick flopping in the breeze. As his second grade Sunday School teacher, I had worked tirelessly to help him memorize ten Bible verses. Josh beamed at the shiny medal encircling his neck, but I knew that his true reward was God's Word implanted in his heart to guide him for the rest of his life.

Lord, thank You for the Bible verses, prayers, and hymns implanted in my heart at a young age. Thank You for how Your Spirit brings them to mind when I need them for encouragement, rebuke, or discernment. Help me to keep increasing the store of truth in my heart. Amen.

PERMISSION TO MOURN

*When I heard this, I sat down and cried. Then for
several days, I mourned; I went without eating
to show my sorrow, and I prayed.*
NEHEMIAH 1:4 CEV

Bad news. When it arrives, what's your reaction? Do you
scream? Fall apart? Run away?

Nehemiah's response to bad news is a model for us. First,
he vented his sorrow. It's okay to cry and mourn. Christians
suffer pain like everyone else—only, we know the source of
inner healing. Disguising our struggle doesn't make us look
more spiritual. . .just less *real.* Like Nehemiah, our next step
is to turn to the only true source of help and comfort.

*Dear God, when You were on earth, You wept. It isn't wrong
to cry; it doesn't mean we don't trust You. It just means
we're human; meant for perfection but living as sinners in
a fallen world. We praise You for knowing us, for being
one of us, for being the God of all comfort. Amen.*

HEALING HEAT

When I am weak, then I am strong.
2 CORINTHIANS 12:10 NASB

As an occupational therapist, I make splints for people with broken bones. The thermoplastic splinting material comes in sheets, hard and unyielding as plywood. When heated, the thermoplastic becomes pliable so it can be cut and molded into a form that promotes healing.

Like that thermoplastic, we're strongest and most usable when we've gone through the melting process. Heat transforms us into moldable beings with which God heals hearts and spirits.

Dear Lord, thank You for the fiery trials in my life which are, even right now, making me more like You. It doesn't feel good to be held over the flame and molded into something different, but, in faith, I know that Your methods are sure and can be trusted. Amen.

PEBBLES

I will give you a new heart and put a new spirit
within you; and I will remove the heart of stone
from your flesh and give you a heart of flesh.
EZEKIEL 36:26 NASB

So many things can harden our hearts: overwhelming loss, shattered dreams; even scar tissue from broken hearts, disillusionment, and disappointment. To avoid pain, we simply turn off feelings. Our hearts become petrified rock—heavy, cold, and rigid. But God can crack our hearts of stone from the inside out and replace that miserable pile of pebbles with soft, feeling hearts of flesh. The amazing result is a brand-new, hope-filled spirit.

Dear Lord, only You can do the work in us of turning
stone to flesh. You give; You put; You remove; You change.
We praise You that You don't leave us with these hard,
dead hearts but give us life through Your Spirit. We praise
You for working in us, even when it hurts. Amen.

DO A LITTLE DANCE

Then Miriam the prophet, Aaron's sister,
took a tambourine and led all the women as
they played their tambourines and danced.

EXODUS 15:20 NLT

Can you imagine the enormous celebration that broke out among the children of Israel when God miraculously saved them from Pharaoh's army at the Red Sea? Even dignified prophetess Miriam grabbed her tambourine and cut loose with her girlfriends. Despite adverse circumstances, she heard God's music and did His dance. Isn't that our goal today? To Hear God's music above the world's cacophony and do His dance as we recognize everyday miracles in our lives?

Lord, loosen my feet to praise You with this body
You have given me! I may look awkward or foolish or
strange, but I just want to praise You with everything
I have. You are worthy of songs, dances, and shouts!
All praise to our amazing, saving God. Amen.

Did You Say Something?

*"Call to Me and I will answer you, and I will tell
you great and mighty things, which you do not know."*
JEREMIAH 33:3 NASB

As someone who's been there, done that, you've gotta love
the commercial where the husband has his face buried in the
newspaper when his wife pops the no-win question: "Does
this dress make me look fat?" "You bet," he distractedly replies.

God promises to not only hear us when we call to Him, but
to answer by teaching us new and amazing things. He's never
distracted. He's always listening. And He always cares.

*Dear Father, thank You for always being there for us,
listening. You are never—as Elijah mocked the prophets
of Baal—asleep or busy or traveling. And You don't just
listen but answer, sometimes even before we call. Thank
You for being the keeper of all answers. Amen.*

PAY DAY

*"Go into all the world and preach
the gospel to all creation."*
Mark 16:15 nasb

One day as our family discussed the Great Commission over dinner, my salesman husband asked my young daughter if she knew what *commission* meant. "Sure," she replied. "It's what you get paid at the end for what you did in the beginning."

Our commission will be paid in heaven when we're surrounded not only by dear friends and family with whom we shared our faith, but also the souls reached by missions we supported with our time, money, and energies.

*Dear Lord, thank You that in Your economy, nothing is
ever wasted: no gift, no prayer, no witness, no sacrifice.
All will contribute to the spread of the Gospel and the
fulfillment of the Great Commission. We praise You for
letting us be a part of Your great work. Amen.*

IT'S NOT OVER

When the wicked die, their hopes die with them,
for they rely on their own feeble strength.

PROVERBS 11:7 NLT

Tony Dungy, Super Bowl champion, coach, and author of *Quiet Strength,* said, "It's because of God's goodness that we can have hope, both for here and the hereafter."

Coach Dungy's testimony of eternal hope for those who rely on God's infinite strength touched many hearts after the tragic loss of his teenage son. Death is not the end. There is a hope, a future for those who choose to *not* rely on their own feeble strength.

Dear God, our own strength is feeble until the moment
when You come in and give us Your strength: to persevere,
to hope, to become more like Jesus. Help us rely on You
and gain the infinite resources of heaven that are always
at our disposal. Praise be to God. Amen.

STREETS OF TREATS

What you hope for is kept safe for you in heaven.
COLOSSIANS 1:5 CEV

Heaven. Will the streets really be paved with gold? Or even better—chocolate? (Have you noticed it's impossible to keep a stash of chocolate safely hidden? Kids can sniff out that stuff like bloodhounds.) No, if our earthly treasures are our source of security and hope, we're in trouble. Rust, thieves, decay, recession. . .*things* just aren't safe. But peace? Joy? Reveling forever in our Lord's presence? All waiting for us safely in heaven. (But who says we can't hope for Godiva-cobbled streets?)

Dear Lord, we long for the sweetness of heaven:
to hear Your voice, to see You face-to-face, to worship at
Your throne with all the saints. That will be sweetness,
indeed, which will never fade. Until then, we thank You
for all the sweetness in our earthly lives. Amen.

SOUL SISTER

"I always see the Lord near me, and I will not be afraid with him at my right side. Because of this, my heart will be glad, my words will be joyful, and I will live in hope."
ACTS 2:25–26 CEV

Laughter is the soul sister of joy; they often travel together. Humor is the primary catalyst for releasing joy into our souls and making our hearts glad. It's healthy for us too! Laughter is cleansing and healing, a powerful salve for the wounds of life. . .a natural medicine and tremendous stress reliever. Laughing is to joy what a 50% OFF sign is to shopping. It motivates us to seek more, more, more!

Dear Father, it is just like You to make something that feels so good also be so good for us. When we laugh, the joy of the Lord becomes our strength—literally. Our muscles, minds, and immune systems are strengthened. Thank You for being our source of joy! Amen.

SMILING HEARTS

Weeping may last for the night, but a
shout of joy comes in the morning.
PSALM 30:5 NASB

What woman hasn't seen the dim underbelly of 2 a.m. through hot tears? God gave us emotionally sensitive spirits and is willing to sit with us as we weep through the long, hard night. Sometimes "night" lasts for a season. But He promises that the sun will eventually rise. And on that glorious morning, we'll be filled with so much joy even our hearts will smile. Joy is appreciated most in the wake of disappointment.

Dear Father, our lives are filled with so many
disappointments: broken relationships, sickness, death,
and loss. But You know just how we feel. Thank You for the
hope of heaven and for the faith to keep looking forward to
that day of unshadowed joy. In love and longing, amen.

Joy: Jesus Occupying You

*May all who fear you find in me a cause
for joy, for I have put my hope in your word.*
PSALM 119:74 NLT

Have you ever met someone you immediately knew was filled with joy? The kind of effervescent joy that bubbles up and overflows, covering everyone around her with warmth and love and acceptance. We love to be near people filled with Jesus-joy. And even more, as Christians we want to be *like* them! Lord, remind us how:

J – Jesus
O – Occupying
Y – You

*Lord, help me not to be jealous of people who have
Your joy. They don't have something that I am missing;
they simply have You. And Your joy is available to me too.
I pray that You would increase my joy by filling me
more and more with Your Holy Spirit. Amen.*

Justice For All?

Our God, you save us, and your fearsome
deeds answer our prayers for justice!
You give hope to people everywhere on earth.
PSALM 65:5 CEV

It's not fair!

How many times have we uttered this indignant cry when life handed us injustice? Our work goes unrecognized; our best efforts are rejected; calamity seems to roost on our doorstep. We demand justice—it's what we deserve, right? But what about all those times we've misstepped or misjudged? James 2:13 tells us that *mercy* triumphs over justice. Mercy forgives mistakes and *doesn't* dole out what is deserved. Mercy—like a jail sentence pardoned. Mercy—like a man on a cross.

Lord, when I am full of a sense of injustice, of having
been wronged by someone or some system, I forget
You. I forget that I am owed nothing; what I actually
deserve is condemnation. Thank You for giving me mercy;
help me to extend that forgiveness to others. Amen.

AS THE TIDE TURNS

*"He will not falter or be discouraged till
he establishes justice on earth. In his
teaching the islands will put their hope."*
ISAIAH 42:4 NIV

Change. . .besides our unalterable Lord, it's the only thing constant in this world. Yet the only person who likes change is a baby with a wet diaper. Isaiah prophesied that the Almighty will one day create positive change on earth. Like the tides that clean beach debris after a storm, positive change washes away the old and refreshes with the new. In this we hope.

*Dearest Lord, You are never discouraged. You never
falter. Your plans always come to pass. Nothing is
outside of Your control. We praise You for who You
are—infinite, incomprehensible, immutable, all-wise.
Your justice is coming. In that Day—and today,
as we hope in You—we will shout AMEN!*

UP IS THE ONLY OUT

Let them lie face down in the dust,
for there may be hope at last.
LAMENTATIONS 3:29 NLT

The Old Testament custom for grieving people was to lie prostrate and cover themselves with ashes. Perhaps the thought was that when you're wallowing in the dust, at least you can't descend any further. There's an element of hope in knowing that, from there, there's only one way to go: up. If a recent loss has you sprawled in the dust, know that God doesn't waste pain in our lives. He will use it for some redeeming purpose.

Dear Father, we thank You for putting us in a position
where our only hope is in You. Thank You for the stones
under our knees and the dust in our nostrils. Thank You
for being right there with us. Thank You for Your voice
in our darkness and Your hand reaching out. Amen.

WELCOME BACK

Train up a child in the way he should go;
and when he is old, he will not depart from it.
PROVERBS 22:6 KJV

I'll never forget the tender bedtime family gatherings on my sister's bed when I was a child. After reading a Bible story from the big picture Bible, we took turns praying. When I had children, I established the same tradition in our home. The Bible promises that if we instill God's Word and principles in our children, they will one day return to it. It may take time, but God's Word will *not* return void.

Dear Lord, we pray today for children who are wandering from the faith. Help us to continue to love them, despite how they may reject us and what we've tried to teach them. Thank You for longing for their salvation even more than we do. In faith and hope, amen.

WHO'S YOUR DADDY?

His name is the Lord.
A father to the fatherless.
PSALM 68:4–5 NIV

His father left when my friend Ben was two. Ben recognized him once—from pictures—at a family funeral, but his father intentionally turned away. When Ben was 35, with a family of his own, his father suddenly showed up, seeking a relationship. Sadly, he was diagnosed with cancer shortly after their reunion and died of cancer within one year. Ben mourned but knew his real paternal relationship was with God, the Father to the fatherless.

Lord, whether our fathers were loving and present or
cruel and absent, we thank You for them because they
gave us life—and therefore, a chance to know and love
You and give our lives to You, our heavenly Father.
Thank You for being our perfect, eternal Father. Amen.

LiVE AND LEARN

Lead me by your truth and teach me, for you are the
God who saves me. All day long I put my hope in you.
PSALM 25:5 NLT

Acquiring spiritual wisdom is a fluid process. Trickles pool into mighty reservoirs from which we draw hope. God is right beside us moment by moment, day by day, guiding us, teaching us, feeding our reservoirs. But if we freeze the Holy Spirit out of our lives by apathetic or indifferent attitudes, the trickle solidifies into ice and the flow of wisdom is blocked. If we keep our minds open to God's everyday lessons, just watch the river surge!

Lord, in Your economy, nothing is wasted. Every moment
of our lives can draw us closer to You or lead us further
astray. Please open our eyes to Your presence in our
lives right now. Please soften our hearts in this moment.
Incline our ears to Your actively speaking voice. Amen.

GETTING TO KNOW YOU

For the law never made anything perfect.
But now we have confidence in a better hope,
through which we draw near to God.
HEBREWS 7:19 NLT

Following Old Testament law used to be considered the way to achieve righteousness, but obeying rules just doesn't work for fallible humans. We mess up. We fail miserably. Then Jesus came and provided a better way to draw near to God. He bridged the gap by offering us a personal relationship rather than rules. Together we laugh, cry, love, grieve, rejoice. We get to *know* our Papa God through our personal relationship with Him.

Dear Father, we are in awe of the fact that You want us to know You, that You care about having a personal relationship with Your creatures. That both humbles and amazes us. Help us to prize that relationship above everything else and to throw off anything that hinders it. Amen.

FRESH AND GREEN

They will still bear fruit in old age,
they will stay fresh and green.
PSALM 92:14 NIV

Doris, a tiny eighty-nine-year-old widow in my Bible study, is teaching me how to be a blessing. That's her prayer every morning of her life: Lord, make me a blessing to someone today. And sure enough, God uses her to touch lives in His name—helping a frantic woman find her lost keys; taking a sick neighbor to the doctor; offering a friendly word to the grumpy, wheelchair-bound man. Little blessings are big indeed to those in need.

Dear Lord, I often think the only works that count are big
ones: converting a lost tribe, translating the Bible into a new
language, preaching a powerful sermon. Forgive me for not
valuing the sphere in which You have placed me. Thank You
for the small song You are teaching me to sing. Amen.

ROCKY ROAD

For through the Spirit we eagerly await by
faith the righteousness for which we hope.
GALATIANS 5:5 NIV

My daughter's five-pound Russian Terror (oops—that's Terrier) is anything but righteous. Rocky dashes after cars, nibbles poisonous plants, and routinely ingests ripped-apart rugs. In order to guide said pup along the path of righteousness, doors must close. The only opened doors invite him to destinations specially prepared for him.

Our paths of righteousness are also guided by the One who shuts doors according to what's best for us. So, girlfriends—enough howling, whining, and scratching at closed doors!

Lord, it's hard to know, sometimes, which is a closed door
and which is a door that requires persistent knocking.
We ask for Your wisdom. Show us what we should do—
and what we should not do. We praise You for both the
open doors and the ones that remain locked. Amen.

NOT SUZIE HOMEMAKER

*The Spirit has given each of us a
special way of serving others.*
1 CORINTHIANS 12:7 CEV

My friend Denise has the gift of hospitality. She welcomes
people into her home and makes them feel loved through her
thoughtful accents: serving food on her best china, lighting
scented candles, offering cozy furnishings. Hospitality is not
my gift. My guests get bagged chips, flat soda, and leave coated
in cat hair. God taught me not to compare and despair, for He
has given each of us our *own* gift to be used for His service.
What's yours?

*God, help me be willing to open my home to other people,
even when it's messy and dirty. Help me open my heart
in a similar way so that they can see my great need
and love for You and the perfect answer found
only in the Gospel of Jesus Christ. Amen.*

SUPERWOMAN ISN'T HOME

*"But we will devote ourselves to prayer
and to the ministry of the word."*
ACTS 6:4 NASB

As busy women, we've found out the hard way that we can't do everything. Heaven knows we've tried, but the truth has found us out: Superwoman is a myth. So we must make priorities and focus on the most important. Prayer and God's Word should be our faith priorities. If we only do as much as we *can* do, then God will take over and do what only He can do. He's got our backs, girls!

*Dear Father, so often I find time to do everything
except pray and read Your Word. Forgive me. Help me
to see the idols and sins that keep me from running
to You daily. Help me to root out even good things if
they are keeping me from You. In Jesus' Name, amen.*

WALKIN' BOOTS

I heard about you from others;
now I have seen you with my own eyes.
JOB 42:5 CEV

As children we sang, "Jesus loves me, this I know; for the Bible tells me so," and we believed because, well, we were told to. But we reach a crossroads as adults: either pull on the boots of faith and take ownership or simply polish them occasionally—maybe at Easter and Christmas—and allow them to sit neglected and dusty in the closet. Have you taken ownership of your faith? Go ahead, sister, those boots were made for walkin'!

Dear Lord, You are the only god who is alive and active, and the more we experience of You, the more real You become. Forgive us for blaming You when we are the ones who have neglected You. Help us build the muscles of our faith through prayer and the Word. Amen.

WORKiNG OUT

I will never give up hope or stop praising you.
PSALM 71:14 CEV

Praise is like a muscle; if we don't exercise it regularly, it becomes weak and atrophied. But if we flex and extend an attitude of gratitude daily, praise grows into a strong, dependable force that nurtures hope and carries us through the worst of circumstances. Like Helen Keller, though blind and deaf, we'll praise our Creator: "I thank God for my handicaps, for through them, I have found myself, my work, and my God."

Dear God, we praise You because we are fearfully and
wonderfully made. Forgive us for the times we have cursed
our weight, our height, our weaknesses, our handicaps,
our personalities. You made us the way we are on purpose
for Your good pleasure. Thank You. Amen.

INEXPLICABLE STRENGTH

"The joy of the LORD is your strength."
NEHEMIAH 8:10 NASB

Joy is not based on the circumstances around us. It is not synonymous with happiness. God promised believers His deep, abiding joy—*not* fleeting happiness, which is here today, gone tomorrow. The joy of the Lord rises above external situations and supernaturally overshadows everything else to become our inexplicable, internal strength.

Dear Father, help us to understand and remember that happiness is fleeting, but joy is at the center of the Trinity— and spreads outward to us. Thank You for being the source of all the joy in the universe. We praise You that Your joy is stronger than anything—even death. Amen.

HE IS ABLE

The prospect of the righteous is joy.
PROVERBS 10:28 NIV

Living joyfully isn't denying reality. The righteous do not receive a "Get Out of Pain Free" card when they place their trust in Christ. We all have hurts in our lives. Some we think we cannot possibly endure. But even in the midst of our darkest times, our heavenly Father is able to reach in with gentle fingers to touch us and infuse us with joy that defies explanation. Impossible? Perhaps by the world's standards. Yet He is *able.*

*Lord, what You ask seems impossible, but we ask You
to make the impossible possible in our lives. We ask for
Your joy in our trials. Only Your Spirit can give us that.
We look to You, just as Jesus looked through the
Cross to the joy set before Him. Amen.*

FOREVER JOY

We don't look at the troubles we can see now. . . .
For the things we see now will soon be gone,
but the things we cannot see will last forever.
2 CORINTHIANS 4:18 NLT

A painter's first brush strokes look like random blobs—
no discernable shape, substance, or clue as to what the com-
pleted painting will be. But in time, the skilled artist brings
order to perceived chaos. Initial confusion is forgotten in joyful admiration of the finished masterpiece.

We often can't see past the blobs of trouble on our life
canvases. We must trust that the Artist has a masterpiece un-
derway. And there will be great joy in its completion.

Dear Lord, we ask for faith to persevere when can't see
the picture You are creating with the circumstances of
our lives. When we doubt, help us look at the glorious
world around us as evidence of Your artistry and
remember that we too are Your handiwork. Amen.

PERFECT LOVE

Love never gives up, never loses faith, is always
hopeful, and endures through every circumstance.
1 CORINTHIANS 13:7 NLT

We have relationships in three directions: upward (with God),
outward (with others), and inward (with ourselves). We are
bound to be disappointed at one time or another by the latter
two. Because of human frailty, we will inevitably experience
failure by others and even ourselves. Our imperfect love will
be strained to the breaking point. But our Creator will never
fail us—His perfect love truly *never* gives up on us.

Father, thank You for Your amazing love. Forgive
us for how we have failed to love You and others;
forgive us for expecting others to love us perfectly
when only You can do that. Help us remain willing to
love and be loved, despite how difficult it is. Amen.

LiGHTHOUSE LOVE

For God who said, "Light shall shine out of darkness,"
is the One who has shone in our hearts.

2 CORINTHIANS 4:6 NASB

Have you heard the story of the lighthouse keeper's daughter who kept faithful vigil for her sailor? Every night she watched as the light's beam pierced the blackness and sliced through raging storms, driven by relentless hope that her lover would return to her on the morning's tide. God loves us like that. He's our light in the darkness, guiding, beckoning, and filling our hearts with hope. He never tires. He never stops.

Almighty God, You are our lighthouse—the light shining
in the darkness, faithfully warning of the rocks and
waves, never failing when the need is greatest. Thank
You for that reminder of who You are. We are tiny and
tempest tossed and need You so much. Amen.

THREE LITTLE WORDS

There are three things that will last
forever—faith, hope, and love.
1 Corinthians 13:13 nlt

Don't you get tired of throwing away panty hose? It's hard to believe that modern technology can scan quivers inside our livers and detect nickel-sized puddles on Mars, but we still can't manufacture hose that won't run. Yep, there are precious few things that endure. Only three, the Bible says. Three things that will never break down, wear out, or get lost. These are the *only* things worth keeping.

Lord, we want to be like You. We want to be little Christs,
here on earth. Our souls will last forever, and we long for
them to be infused with faith, hope, and love. That seems
like a tall order some days. We ask for Your Spirit
to fill us and do what we can't do. Amen.

NEW LIFE

God is so good, and by raising Jesus from death,
he has given us new life and a hope that lives on.
1 PETER 1:3 CEV

The words of a song I wrote while pregnant with my first child exult in the similarities between new physical life and new spiritual life in Christ: "New life stirs within me now. Like a soft breeze, transforming me now. It's a miracle of love, precious blessing from above. My heart has taken wings. . .lift me up!"

New life. By the goodness of God, we can experience this precious transformation no less miraculous than a baby growing within us.

Lord, when I look back on who I once was it gives me great
hope for who I will become through Your transforming
power. By Your grace, I am a new creation. Just as parents
help their children grow until they can spread wings
and fly, so You are lifting me. Amen.

TIMEOUT

The LORD will not abandon His people.
1 SAMUEL 12:22 NASB

Do you remember when, as a little girl, you languished alone in your room as punishment? Or maybe you sat with your nose plastered to the corner in timeout. It felt like your parents had abandoned you, didn't it? As adults, we sometimes *feel* abandoned when that's not the case at all. We're actually in a place strategically chosen by a loving Father to teach us, broaden us, and improve us in the end.

Dear Father, You are growing me all the time, in every situation. Through pain, tears, triumph, and even the humdrum of everyday life. Help me believe that, even when I feel alone. You are there; You are with me in all things. You will never leave me. Amen.

THAT MORNING

You have placed your faith and hope in God because he raised Christ from the dead and gave him great glory.
1 PETER 1:21 NLT

Have you ever wondered how Mary felt that Easter morning when she discovered Jesus' tomb empty? Already grieving, imagine the shock of discovering the body of her Savior—the One who held all her hopes and dreams—gone! How can that be? Maybe. . . ? Hope glimmers. But no—impossible. He *did* say something about resurrection, but that was figurative, wasn't it? Who are. . . *It's You?* I must run to tell them. It's true! He has risen! He's alive! My hope lives too!

Dear Father, we praise You that You did not let Your Holy One see decay, that the grave could not contain Him! Jesus is alive! And because He lives, I can too. I praise You that I do not need to fear death because it is the gateway to eternal life. Amen.

PATIENCE OF HOPE

We call to mind your work of faith, your labor of love, and your patience of hope in following our Master, Jesus Christ, before God our Father.

1 THESSALONIANS 1:3 MSG

Labor. The word alone draws a shudder from the most stalwart of pregnant women. Just as laboring to bring forth new physical life requires patience, birthing new spiritual life may require an intensive labor of love: ceaseless prayer. Countless mothers on their knees praying for the salvation of a loved one have rejoiced in answered prayer. Their secret? *Patience of hope.*

Dear Lord, I praise You for the miracle of prayer: that You ask me to approach You in this way, and that Your ear is always turned in my direction. Thank You that when I pray for my child, You answer by changing us both. Who is like You, working miracles? Amen.

131

BIGGER AND BETTER

*Waiting does not diminish us, any more than waiting
diminishes a pregnant mother. We are enlarged in
the waiting. We, of course, don't see what is enlarging
us. But the longer we wait, the larger we become,
and the more joyful our expectancy.*

Romans 8:24–25 MSG

Life is filled with waiting—on slow people, transportation, doctor reports, even for God to act. Waiting often requires patience we don't have. It feels like perpetual pregnancy—anticipating a baby that is never delivered. The secret is to clasp hands with our Lord. He offers His shield of protection from sinful attitudes like impatience, irritability, and anger and replaces them with self-control, kindness, and even joy.

Waiting is inevitable, but we can draw closer to the Father in the waiting.

*God, I confess that I don't like to wait; I want results
now. Help me be more like You; let my longing enlarge
me and enlarge my sense of You. You are as big as
eternity and as patient as forever. Show me how to
be both content and joyfully expectant. Amen.*

WAiT JUST A MiNUTE

We wait in hope for the LORD;
he is our help and our shield.
PSALM 33:20 NIV

Impatience: archenemy of women. Like Batman's Riddler, or Superman's Lex Luther, impatience stalks us, plots our demise, and blindsides us via thoughtless neighbors, inconsiderate drivers, careless clerks, dense husbands, children taking for–ev–er. But waiting is an unavoidable part of life, and the Bible says we don't have to be undone by it. The Lord's patience is our shield and defense, and He's got plenty stockpiled.

Father, we know Your Word says the plans You have for us
are to help us, not to harm us. So. . .that means the slow
drivers, the frustrating relatives, the inconsiderate people
who remind us that we are not the center of the universe—
that's Your plan too. Thank You. Amen.

PLEASE RESCUE ME

I long for you to rescue me!
Your word is my only hope.
PSALM 119:81 CEV

Have you ever longed to be rescued?

Stranded after shredding knee ligaments during a remote mountain skiing accident, I waited helplessly for rescuers to arrive. All alone on the raw Canadian mountainside, I felt fear mount. Freezing temperatures, prowling cougars, and unrelenting pain threatened to engulf me in despair. So I did the most and the least I could do: I prayed and recited scripture. And my faithful heavenly Father rescued me with His peace.

Dear Father, thank You for all the times You have rescued
me from trouble and temptation. Thank You for the times
You have rescued me from dangers I wasn't even aware of.
Thank You for being with me now. Rescue is coming,
if not today or tomorrow, then in eternity. Amen.

GUILT-FREE

*"I will forgive their wickedness, and I will
never again remember their sins."*
HEBREWS 8:12 NLT

Guilt. It tends to consume us women to the point that ninety percent of the things we do are motivated by guilt. But God says we don't have to allow guilt to control us. We should learn from past mistakes, certainly, and then shed the guilt like a moth-eaten winter coat. Don a fresh spring outfit and look ahead. Our past prepares us for the future if we are open to the present.

*Dear Lord, forgive me for holding on to my mistakes and
wallowing in guilt—as if You had only covered some of
my sins with Your forgiveness. Thank You for what my
sins have shown me about myself and my choices; thank
You for washing me whiter than snow. Amen.*

CLiMB IN

May the God of hope fill you with all joy and peace
as you trust in him, so that you may overflow
with hope by the power of the Holy Spirit.

ROMANS 15:13 NIV

Trust is the bottom line when it comes to living an abundant life. We will never escape the muddy ruts without trusting that God has the leverage and power to pull us out of the quagmire. They say faith is like believing the tight rope walker can cross the gorge pushing a wheelbarrow. Trust is climbing into his wheelbarrow. Only when we climb into God's wheelbarrow can His joy and peace overflow as hope into our hearts.

Lord, often what we see in front of us seems impossible.
We can't see any way out. But we thank You that when
things seem impossible, that is when we see You most
clearly at work. Help us trust You when the way ahead
looks as daunting as a high wire. Amen.

HOPE RESURRECTED

We had hoped that he would be the one
to set Israel free! But it has already been
three days since all this happened.
LUKE 24:21 CEV

The scenario for this scripture is quite unusual. Two of Jesus' disciples are describing their lost hope due to the events surrounding Jesus' death to none other than Jesus Himself. They don't recognize Him as they walk together on the road to Emmaus after His resurrection. Spiritual cataracts blind them to the hope they thought was dead—right in front of them!

Let's open our spiritual eyes to Jesus, who is walking beside us.

God, we laugh at the disciples, complaining to the
Risen Lord that He wasn't who they had hoped He was!
We think we would have had more discernment if we were
in their shoes. But without Your Spirit, we are equally
blind. Please open our eyes to Your nearness now. Amen.

SPROUTS

"For there is hope for a tree, when it
is cut down, that it will sprout again."
JOB 14:7 NASB

Have you ever battled a stubborn tree? You know, one you can saw off at the ground but the tenacious thing keeps sprouting new growth from the roots? You have to admire the resiliency of that life-force, struggling in its refusal to give up. That's hope in a nutshell, sisters. We must believe, even as stumps, that we will eventually become majestic, towering evergreens if we just keep sending out those sprouts.

Dear Lord, only You really know how often I struggle,
then give up, only to muster up hope and try again.
That perseverance can only come from You. Thank You
for not allowing me to give up. And I long for the
day when I will flourish in Your presence. Amen.

COUNTING ON IT

Blessed is the one who perseveres under trial because,
having stood the test, that person will receive the crown
of life that the Lord has promised to those who love him.
JAMES 1:12 NIV

Some think that when you turn your life over to Christ, troubles are over. But if you've been a believer for more than a day, you'll realize that the Christian life is no Caribbean cruise. There will be trials; there will be tribulations. Count on it. But Jesus promises a glorious reward for our perseverance through those hard times. Count on *that* even more.

Lord, I know that nothing in this life is perfect, and even
if I went on a Caribbean cruise, there'd probably be
a storm at sea, E. coli in the lettuce, or. . .pirates. Only
heaven—because it's Your dwelling—is perfect.
Thank You for what waits for me in eternity. Amen.

SPRUNG

*Because of the covenant I made with you, sealed
with blood, I will free your prisoners from death in
a waterless dungeon. Come back to the place of
safety, all you prisoners who still have hope!*
ZECHARIAH 9:11–12 NLT

In the marvelous movie, *The Count of Monte Cristo*, Edmond
Dantes (played by Jim Caviezel) is unjustly imprisoned in the
darkest of dungeons—bitter, hopeless, helpless. Against all
odds, God enables him to escape and eventually return victorious, a hope-filled man.

Have you ever felt trapped in a prison of hopelessness?
Financial difficulties, poor health, unemployment, rocky marriage, delinquent children—there are countless dungeons that
shackle us. But God promises hope and freedom from our
prisons. Jesus bailed us out!

*Dear Lord, thank You for the freedom we now have in
Christ. Sin and death have been defeated, and we wait
only for Your second coming to see all made right.
Until then, thank You for the gift of the Spirit, which is
making us new creations. Come, Lord Jesus! Amen.*

OVERFLOWING LOVE

Precious in the sight of the LORD
is the death of His godly ones.
PSALM 116:15 NASB

Jesus wept.

Two small words that portray the enormity of Jesus' emotion following the death of His dear friend, Lazarus (John 11:35). Jesus knew Lazarus wouldn't stay dead, that he'd soon miraculously rise from the grave. So why did Jesus weep? The depth of His love for those precious to Him overflowed. Our Lord grieves with us in our losses today and comforts us with the knowledge that His beloved will rise to eternal life in heaven.

Lord, I am comforted to see that death is a horror
to You too. It is wrong; it is ugly; it was not part of
Your plan. You also long for the day when death's
tentacles will be unwrapped from Your beautiful
world, and we will all live together forever. Amen.

POWER SOURCE

He gives strength to the weary and
increases the power of the weak.
ISAIAH 40:29 NIV

Sometimes we feel as if our backs will break under the burdens we carry: debt, responsibilities, impossible schedules. But our God promises to strengthen and empower us if we turn to Him for help. He knows. He cares. He is able.

It's been written that persecuted European Christians don't pray for God to lessen their loads like American Christians do. They pray for stronger backs instead.

Lord, we pray for discernment to know which of the
burdens we carry are from You and which we have
picked up on our own. We pray to be strong enough to
carry the ones You have given and also strong enough
to leave behind the ones that are not from You. Amen.

No Call-Waiting

Call on me and come and pray to me,
and I will listen to you.
JEREMIAH 29:12 NIV

"I will listen to you." Every woman's dream.

Jeremiah knew the importance of being listened to. He proclaimed God's message for forty years to the unseeing, unhearing, unresponsive nation of Judah. His ironic good news: God is listening!

Do you ever feel like no one's listening? The Bible says God hears us every time we utter His name. How precious we are to our Creator that He bends His omnipotent ear each time we call on Him.

Dear God, thank You that we don't need to shout for
You to respond. Thank You for hearing us when we are
too troubled even to form words. You understand groans,
sobs, whimpers, shrieks. Help us to call on You more and
more; thank You for always listening. Amen.

JUICED

God is our refuge and strength,
a very present help in trouble.
PSALM 46:1 NASB

Remember the scene from the movie *Air Force One*, when Harrison Ford, as the US President, calls for help from the belly of a terrorist-hijacked plane after much death-defying effort? Just as the crucial call is dialed, his cell phone battery conks out. Can you identify? What a relief that our direct line to God—prayer—is always juiced and never needs recharging!

Dear Father, we confess all the things we rely on apart from You: people, circumstances, talents, possessions. Only You are omnipresent and omnipotent—always ready and always able. Everything else will fail us. We praise You, our refuge and our strength, our very present help in trouble. Amen.

CLOSE TO YOU

I stay close to you, and your
powerful arm supports me.
PSALM 63:8 CEV

There's an old saying: "I used to be close to God, but someone moved." If God is the same yesterday, today, and tomorrow, He's not the one going anywhere. So how do we stay close to God? So close that His powerful arm supports, protects, and lifts us up when we're down? Prayer: as a lifestyle, as much a part of ourselves as breathing. Prayer isn't just spiritual punctuation; it's every word of our life story.

Dear Lord, forgive me for the times I have forgotten
to pray. . .when I've been busy, preoccupied, or intent
on doing things on my own. I long to live under Your
powerful, protective arm. Teach me daily to turn to
You and guide me into a lifestyle of prayer. Amen.

Slip-Sliding Away

Instruct those who are rich in this present world not to be
conceited or to fix their hope on the uncertainty of riches,
but on God, who richly supplies us with all things to enjoy.
1 Timothy 6:17 nasb

My friend Claire lived large with a millionaire husband, enormous house, designer clothes, and flashy convertible—even a cook (to my envy!). But suddenly, the economy plunged south, and in the twinkle of a bank vault key, she lost it all. Divorced, homeless, and bitter, Claire was forced to wait tables to pay her ill son's medical bills. We can't depend on money—here today, gone tomorrow. Our hope must be fixed on our eternal God.

Dear Father, You give us good gifts in this life to enjoy,
but we always forget—first, that they come from You and
second, that they are fleeting. Forgive our shortsightedness.
Nothing will survive death except our own souls. Thank You
for teaching us by both giving and taking away. Amen.

PRioRiTiES

Let all that you do be done in love.
1 Corinthians 16:14 nasb

Sometimes we get so wrapped up in our daily to-do lists that we put our duties above people. "Leave me alone until this project is finished, kids." "Sorry, Sue, I'm too busy to have lunch." "Oh, I don't have time to talk to Mom today; I'll let the answering machine get it."

How, then, can we ever share the love of Christ with those we've shoved out of our way? People don't care how much you know until they know how much you care.

Lord, I am guilty of this every day, in one way or another. I long to be like You and patiently welcome people with no agenda but love. Help me put aside all that I think I have to do and be willing to sit, listen, and share Your love. Amen.

ONE NATION UNDER GOD

The poor are filled with hope,
and injustice is silenced.
JOB 5:16 CEV

"Give me your tired, your poor, your huddled masses. . . ." beckons the Statue of Liberty, offering a home and freedom to hurting people. Many of our ancestors flocked to American shores that were offering freedom of worship and an end to the injustice of religious persecution. May we never forget the sacrifices they made to pursue the hope of providing their children—you and me—with a nation founded on Christian principles. Let's strive to preserve that hope for future generations.

Dear God, we are blessed to live in a peaceful, fruitful
country with a long history of honoring You. Forgive us
for how we've strayed from You and how those of us who
still believe have been silent in the face of sin and injustice.
Open our lips; ready our feet for action. Amen.

A STRONG TOWER

The name of the LORD is a fortified tower;
the righteous run to it and are safe.

<small>PROVERBS 18:10 NIV</small>

We of the twenty-first century tend to limit our references to God, but ancient Hebrew translations offer a broader perspective. There is intrinsic hope in the names of God: *Elohim* (Mighty Creator), *El Olam* (The Everlasting God), *Yahweh Yireh* (The Lord Will Provide), *Yahweh Shalom* (The Lord Is Peace), *Yahweh Tsuri* (The Lord, My Rock), and *Abba* (Father) to name a few. Let's broaden our scope of His powerful name in our prayers today.

Dear God, all those names are not just descriptions
of You but solid, actual truth—the Word made flesh.
We praise and thank You for who You are. We trust
in all of Your names; they are all true, all the time,
for all people, in all places. Who is like You? Amen.

24-7

He will not let your foot slip—he who
watches over you will not slumber.
PSALM 121:3 NIV

I love hiking the winding mountain paths near our remote Smoky Mountain cabin. Sometimes I get so caught up in watching hummingbirds or admiring cliff-side vistas that I stumble, forgetting that inattention could be deadly. How comforting to know that our Lord is *always* alert as He watches over us. We don't have to worry that an important prayer will slip by while He sneezes or that He'll nap through our surgery. He's always on duty.

Dear Lord, thank You for Your ever-watchful,
loving care of us. Thank You for guiding our steps and
our prayers and for steadying us, even when we were
unaware we were about to fall. We trust You; we love
You; we marvel that Your eyes are always on us. Amen.

PAPA GOD

And he did it, rescued us from certain doom.
And he'll do it again, rescuing us as
many times as we need rescuing.
2 CORINTHIANS 1:10 MSG

"Don't touch!" Lauren scolded her toddler who was reaching for the electrical cord. "No!" Lauren grabbed the nickel from little Erin's hand as it headed toward her mouth. "Always hold Mommy's hand!" Lauren reminded Erin as she dashed for the street. Mothers repeatedly rescue children from dangers they can't comprehend. Likewise, our heavenly Father rescues us from unforeseen consequences. Breathe a grateful prayer today.

Dear Father, I know that the only reason I am sitting here
today, praying, is because of Your unseen hand protecting
me. I made so many foolish choices in the past that could
have led me to far different places, and I am eternally
grateful for Your watchful shepherding. Amen.

ONE GUTSY GAL

*"It could be that you were made
queen for a time like this!"*
ESTHER 4:14 CEV

Crowned queen after winning a beauty contest, Esther was
only allowed audience with her king when summoned. A wave
of his scepter would pardon her from execution, but he was a
hard man—and unpredictable. When Esther learned of a plot
to destroy her people, she faced a tough decision. She was
the *only* one who could save them—at supreme risk. God had
intentionally placed her in that position for that time. What's
your divinely ordained position?

*Lord, my divinely ordained position is simply where
You have placed me right now. Esther didn't have to do
anything except what was right in front of her at that
moment. But it was hard, Lord. And dangerous. Give me
the courage to act when and how You desire. Amen.*

Cool Summer Shower

*"He will renew your life and
sustain you in your old age."*
RUTH 4:15 NIV

Ruth's blessing of renewal is applicable to us today. *Renovatio* is Latin for "rebirth." It means casting off the old and embracing the new: a revival of spirit, a renovation of attitude. Something essential for women to espouse every day of their lives. Like a cool rain shower on a sizzling summer day, Ruth's hope was renewed by her Lord's touch, and ours will be too, if we look to Him for daily replenishing.

*Dear Father, we try to find renewal in so many ways,
but true renewal only comes from You. Thank You
that Your refreshing can come in the midst of heartache,
suffering, waiting—You are larger than any of those
things. Fill us, Lord, with the balm of Your Spirit. Amen.*

RAISING OUR HOPES

"Did I ask you for a son, my lord?" she said.
"Didn't I tell you, 'Don't raise my hopes'?"
2 KINGS 4:28 NIV

Are you afraid to raise your hope in God's provision for fear
that hope will crash and burn? The woman from Shunem had
everything but her heart's desire—a child. She was afraid to
believe Elisha's prediction of her pregnancy but his prayerful
intervention made her dream come true. When the boy later
died, however, she lashed out. God restored her son and raised
her hope from the dead. Literally. Dare we raise our hopes too?

Dear Lord, everything that comes from You is for our
good—the yes and the no. You both give and take away,
but never out of spite, never to torment us. Help us to
trust Your goodness, always—when You give us our
heart's desire and when You do not. Amen.

ZOMBIE ZONE

Be joyful in hope, patient in
affliction, faithful in prayer.
ROMANS 12:12 NIV

Affliction has a tendency to suck the joy right out of our lives, leaving us stranded in the dully-funks. You know—that black hole of existence where our minds fog, emotions go numb, eyes glaze over, and we languish in a state of spiritual dullness. A spiritual zombie zone. But if we're faithful in prayer, God will be faithful to rescue us from those joy-sucking dully-funks and fill us to the brim with His abundant joy.

Dear Lord, when my mind is cloudy and sluggish and
joy seems lost, help me remember the Gospel. Help me
to preach it to myself, so that the joy set before Jesus
at the Cross once again becomes the joy set before me.
Remind me to confide in Your listening ear. Amen.

DIVINE REFRESHMENT

*You were tired out by the length of your road,
yet you did not say, "It is hopeless." You found
renewed strength, therefore you did not faint.*
ISAIAH 57:10 NASB

By the end of each day, most women are ready to collapse. Tight schedules, relentless deadlines, and plaguing debts make our daily roads not just physically tiring but spiritually draining. Our reserves border on empty. How encouraging to know that renewed strength is available through the fountain that never runs dry. If we fill our buckets with living water—Bible reading, Christian music, inspirational books and DVDs—we will not faint, but enjoy divine refreshment.

*God, many of the things I do please You, but—
if I'm honest—I know many don't. Please give me
wisdom to choose the best. You say Your yoke is easy
and Your burden is light, and I believe that. Give me
the discipline to make it true in my life. Amen.*

NONSTICK ATTITUDES

A joyful heart is good medicine.
<small>PROVERBS 17:22 NASB</small>

Laughter is to hope as nonstick cooking spray is to a shiny new muffin tin: It keeps the goo from sticking. Once the batter of everyday responsibility hardens and adheres to our attitudes, it's awfully hard to scrape off enough crust for hope to shine through. But if we coat our day with a little laughter and the joy of the Lord, problems will slide off a lot better. And hope sparkles.

Dear God, please help us to so firmly fix our eyes on Jesus that the problems of this life grow dim in comparison. There is no one else for us! Your joy is our strength and song, our joy and delight. Please help us sing with conviction in these messy, crummy days. Amen.

TWO-STRANDED ROPE

The widow who is really in need and left all
alone puts her hope in God and continues night
and day to pray and to ask God for help.
1 Timothy 5:5 niv

Some women feel as though they are irreparably weakened when they are widowed. Where there once were three strands of a sturdy rope (his, hers, and God's), there now are two. But those who persevere through faith and true grit say the secret is to learn to rejoice in what's left instead of lamenting what has been lost. Look forward. Move forward. Keep that two-stranded rope strong, and never lose hope of a better tomorrow.

Dear Lord, when we are down, give us Your joy; when we
are hopeless, give us Your hope; when we are in pain,
give us Your patience; when we are tired, give us Your
renewal. We can do all things through You, and we
praise You for Your ministering Spirit. Amen.

GLIMMERING GOLD

*"So in everything, do to others what
you would have them do to you."*
MATTHEW 7:12 NIV

The Golden Rule. Most of us were raised with this basic guide
to human relations, but sometimes the message gets turned
around. Instead, we follow the Nedlog (golden backward) Rule:
Don't do for others because they don't do for you. But Jesus
didn't say repay in kind; He said pay forward. The actions of
others are irrelevant. Regardless of what others do, we should
treat them the way we'd like to be treated: with respect and
consideration.

*Dear Lord, we don't have to keep tabs on what we are
owed because You have already paid the debt. Nothing
is owing; all is a gift. We thank You for our salvation
and pray that we would be as free with our love and
forgiveness as You have been to us. Amen.*

BET THE FARM

*Whoever plows and threshes should be able
to do so in the hope of sharing in the harvest.*
1 Corinthians 9:10 NIV

There's a young man who works in children's church with me
who is loud, brash, impulsive, an incessant talker, and loves the
Lord with all his heart. The kids think he's hilarious. I think
he's obnoxious. But I must remind myself that God uses him
in unique ways to reach young hearts with the gospel that I
never could. He's a plowman and I'm a thresher, and we work
together to harvest souls into God's kingdom.

*Lord, when I think of the Body of Christ, I often silently
give thanks that I'm not a toe. . .or some unmentionable
part. But without toes, how could we walk? There are
humble parts we simply cannot do without. Forgive my
pride, Lord. We are all valuable in Your sight. Amen.*

THE SALVAGE MASTER

We are pressed on every side by troubles, but we are not crushed. We are perplexed, but not driven to despair.
2 CORINTHIANS 4:8 NLT

Many women struggle with depression at some point in their lives: post-partum, kids-partum (empty nest), brain-partum (menopause), and anytime in between. We feel that we are being compressed into a rock-hard cube like the product of a trash compactor. The normal details of life suddenly become perplexing and overwhelming. But God does not abandon us to the garbage dump. He is the Salvage Master and recycles us into sterling images of His glory.

Dear Lord, when my mind is foggy or low, let me press into You for clarity and comfort. You promise both. You promise I will not be crushed or driven to despair. Help me persevere in reading Your Word and prayer until You answer. He who promises is faithful. Amen.

MAKEOVER

Since I was worse than anyone else, God had
mercy on me and let me be an example
of the endless patience of Christ Jesus.
1 TIMOTHY 1:16 CEV

Saul was a Jesus-hater. He went out of his way to hunt down believers to torture, imprison, and kill. Yet Christ tracked *him* down and confronted him in a blinding light on a dusty road. Saul's past no longer mattered. Previous sins were forgiven and forgotten. He was given a fresh start. A life makeover. We too, are offered a life makeover. Christ offers to create a beautiful new image of Himself in us, unblemished and wrinkle-free.

Dear Lord, thank You that when we first come to You
in repentance, You forgive our sins and forget them—
completely. They are gone, drowned in Your mercy.
We praise You that Your forgiveness is so deep and
wide. Thank You for making us over. Amen.

WiNGS

*This means that anyone who belongs to
Christ has become a new person. The old
life is gone; a new life has begun!*
2 CORINTHIANS 5:17 NLT

Have you ever seen a butterfly crawling on her belly with
caterpillars? Or trying desperately to hang on to her cocoon
as she takes to the skies? Of course not—she spreads her
wings and flies far away from her old life, discovering new
and wonderful things she never knew existed.

New life in Christ is full of discoveries and wonders, but
you can't get there if you're still clutching the old life. It's time
to let go, sister.

*Dear Father, thank You for offering me a completely new life
in Christ. I don't have to hold on to the past; it has no hold on
me. Help me to see where I am clutching things You want me
to put down. Open my hands so that You can fill them. Amen.*

LOOK TO THE SUNRISE

I rise before dawn and cry for help;
I have put my hope in your word.
PSALM 119:147 NIV

Could be stress or worry or berserk hormones. Whatever the cause, many women find themselves staring at their dark bedroom ceilings in the wee morning hours. We try counting sheep, but they morph into naughty little children, and we exhaust ourselves chasing them through fitful dreams. We're tormented by the *what if's*, guilted by the *should have's*, and jolted wider awake by the *don't forget to's*. But a new day is dawning and help is but a prayer away.

Lord, when I wake in the night, assaulted by worry,
help me to take my eyes off myself and turn them to Jesus.
Fill my mind with thanksgiving; fill my heart with praise;
fill my mouth with prayers to the living, listening God.
Both sleeping and waking are gifts from You. Amen.

DESERT OASIS

Yes, my soul, find rest in God;
my hope comes from him.
PSALM 62:5 NIV

Rest. Far too elusive in our world of bustling busyness. Overwhelming responsibilities run us ragged. We find ourselves not just physically frazzled, but bankrupt of spirit. Exhaustion steals our joy.

Like an oasis in the desert, our Father offers rest for our weary souls and restores our hope. He helps us unload our burdens, relax beside His still waters, and drink in the sparkling refreshment of truth.

Lord, forgive us for so often putting You last on our
to-do list. Forgive us for reading Your Word or praying
when we have the time, instead of putting You first.
Help us to realize that our days are gifts from You
and to find rest in You before anything else. Amen.

CHiLL

I lie awake thinking of you, meditating on you
through the night. Because you are my helper,
I sing for joy in the shadow of your wings.

PSALM 63:6–7 NLT

Are you a worrier? Do you frequently find yourself working up a sweat building molehills into mountains during the midnight hours? This passage suggests an alternative for that nasty and unproductive habit. Instead of worrying, try meditating on the loving-kindness of God. Like a distressed chick tucked safely beneath the snug wings of the mother hen, allow the joy of being loved and protected to relax your tense muscles and ease you into peaceful rest.

Dear Lord, thank You for the example of David. He had
so many things to worry him, yet he meditated on You
when he couldn't sleep. He praised You when his soul
was hurting. Despite the dangers, he danced before You.
Help me to live like that, even in the darkness. Amen.

SHOWERS OF BLESSING

Do the skies themselves send down showers?
No, it is you, LORD our God. Therefore our hope
is in you, for you are the one who does all this.
JEREMIAH 14:22 NIV

Have you ever stood in your parched garden, praying for rain? The plants you've nurtured from seeds are wilting, flower petals litter the ground, fruit withers on the vine. Then thunder clouds roll and the skies burst forth with reinvigorating rain.

There will be dry times too, in our spiritual gardens, when drought threatens to shrivel our faith. But our hope is in the Lord our God, who sends showers to revive us. Deluge us today, Lord.

Dear Lord, You send heat and cold, rain and dry winds.
Since nothing is outside Your control, we can thank
You for the rain showers and for the dry times.
Help us to rejoice in the rain and persevere in the
droughts. Our lives are in Your hands. Amen.

SNIPPETS of HOPE

I also pray that you will understand the incredible greatness of God's power for us who believe him. This is the same mighty power that raised Christ from the dead and seated him in the place of honor at God's right hand in the heavenly realms.

EPHESIANS 1:19–20 NLT

Daydreams are snippets of hope for our souls. Yearnings for something better, something more exciting, something that lifts our spirits. Some dreams are mere fancy, but others are meant to last a lifetime because God embedded them in our hearts. It's when we lose sight of those dreams that hope dies.

But God offers us access to His almighty power—the very same greatness that brought His Son back from the dead. What greater hope is there?

God, thank You for the dreams You have given me— both the ones that have come true and the ones that still glimmer in the distance. Thank You for how they give me hope. But help me place my eternal hope not on those dreams but on You, the dream-giver. Amen.

TRUE SUCCESS

"For I know the plans I have for you,"
declares the LORD, "plans to prosper you and not
to harm you, plans to give you hope and a future."
JEREMIAH 29:11 NIV

As little girls, we dream about the handsome man we'll one day marry, exciting trips we'll take, the mansion we'll call home, and the beautiful, perfect children we'll have. A *successful* life— isn't that what we hope for?

But God doesn't call us to be successful; He calls us to trust Him. We may never be successful in the world's eyes, but trust in our Father's omnipotence ensures our future and our hope. And that's true success.

Lord, Your promises are sure. We can rest in them.
Thank You so much for Your Word, which repeats those
promises over and over in different ways to ensure that
we get it: we have a hope and a future! And because
You have already won the victory, we have too. Amen.

I CAN'T LOSE!

Alive, I'm Christ's messenger; dead, I'm his bounty.
Life versus even more life! I can't lose.
PHILIPPIANS 1:21 MSG

The old timer smiled at his granddaughter as she rebuked him for driving the farm tractor. "Don't you know the danger at your age, Grandpa? You could be killed!"

"I'm not worried, darlin', and you shouldn't be either. What's the worst that could happen? I wake up in heaven. This life versus an even better one. . .for all eternity."

When worry begins to overshadow hope, remember three little words from Philippians: I can't lose!

Lord, Paul said it too: "To live is Christ and to die is gain." Help me to live like that, rejoicing in this beautiful life You have given and in the glorious life to come. I don't know how to strike that balance, so I ask for Your wisdom and guidance. Amen.

ACCOLADES

*Your Father, who sees what is done
in secret, will reward you.*
MATTHEW 6:4 NIV

The countless things we women do for our families are often not noticed or appreciated. What a comfort to know that our Father sees *everything*, no matter how small. Our reward may not be the Woman of the Year award, or even hugs and kisses. It may not be here on earth at all. I'm hoping it'll be a maid and cook for all eternity. But whatever it is, we'll be *thrilled* because our Father is pleased with us.

Dear Lord, thank You for the family You have given me to love and serve. Forgive me for the times when I have craved their approval more than Yours. Forgive me for doing my good deeds so others will notice. You see; You notice; You are pleased. And that is enough. Amen.

EASY AS ABC

God has done all this, so that we will look for him and
reach out and find him. He isn't far from any of us.
ACTS 17:27 CEV

God is near. But we must reach out for Him. There's a line that
we choose to cross, a specific action we take. We can't ooze
into the kingdom of God; it's an intentional decision. It's simple, really—as simple as ABC. A is *Admitting* we're sinful and
in need of a Savior. B is *Believing* that Jesus died for our sins
and rose from the grave. C is *Committing* our lives to Him. Life
everlasting is then ours.

Dear Lord, I admit I'm a sinner. I believe that Jesus died for my
sins and rose from the grave. I commit my life to Him. There's
nothing complicated about that prayer; a child could pray it.
Thank You for being as near as those three words. Amen.

BESTSELLER

The mystery is that Christ lives in you,
and he is your hope of sharing in God's glory.
COLOSSIANS 1:27 CEV

Everybody loves a good mystery—as long as the plot twists a bit and the good guy wins in the end. The Christian life is a mystery. It's baffling that God could love us so deeply that He sent His only Son to suffer and die for us. And now the risen Christ lives in our hearts, bridging the gap between us and God forever. What an incredible page-turner!

Dear Father, we don't understand at all why You love us
so much. But thank You from the bottom of our hearts.
We deserve nothing, but You have given us everything,
forever. We praise Your holy, loving, generous,
faithful, mysterious, glorious Name. Amen.

BEAUTiFY

For the LORD takes pleasure in His people;
He will beautify the afflicted ones with salvation.
PSALM 149:4 NASB

My friend Anna is beautiful. The fact that she's suffered a stroke is insignificant. Her sweet spirit of faithfulness, generosity, and kindness, all couched in gentle humor, causes me to take pleasure in her company.

In the same way, our Lord takes pleasure in our company, despite our inabilities, unsightliness, or neediness. Hard to believe He actually *chooses* our company, but He does! And in spending time with us, He beautifies us with His lovely countenance.

Dear Father, the world tells us that we need to buy
something to be beautiful, but You tell us that we
are beautiful just because You made us and love us.
Thank You for choosing us and loving us so unexpectedly.
Thank You that You take pleasure in us. Amen.

SURVIVOR

The terrible storm raged for many days,
blotting out the sun and the stars,
until at last all hope was gone.
ACTS 27:20 NLT

Following a lovely renewal of our wedding vows on our tenth anniversary, my husband and I boarded a Caribbean cruise ship. Tragically, Hurricane Gilbert obliterated our destination, Cancun, before hurling our ship back and forth on twelve-foot waves for four interminable days. I felt hopeless, sick as a pup, and at the mercy of the storm.

Life's like that, isn't it? Unexpected storms blow up, blot out the light, and toss us about. But we are survivors!

Dear Lord, thank You for keeping us safe in that
storm—and in other storms since then. Thank You
for being with us in the wind and waves, for promising
never to leave us alone. We praise You for being the
God who commands the wind and the waters. Amen.

LiViNG HOPE

*Now faith is confidence in what we hope
for and assurance about what we do not see.*
HEBREWS 11:1 NIV

This beloved scripture has long been the Christian's definition
of faith. But if reworked a smidge, it's also the meaning of hope
in Christ: hope is being sure of in whom we have placed our
faith and certain of what we do not see. We don't see fragrance
or love or blood flowing through our bodies, but we're certain
of their existence. We can't see hope, but there's no doubt when
it's alive within us. Praise God for living hope!

*Dear Father, thank You for reminding us on whom our hope
rests: Jesus, who both embodies, inspires, and guarantees
our hope. Hope seems invisible, intangible, and fragile,
but, through Christ, it is stronger and more enduring than
anything we face. We praise the author of hope. Amen.*

BAND-AiDS

*We have run to God for safety. Now his promises
should greatly encourage us to take hold
of the hope that is right in front of us.*

HEBREWS 6:18 CEV

Have you ever lost your glasses or your keys and looked everywhere for them, only to have someone point out that they're right in front of you? God's hope is like that—right in front of us, but we don't always see it. Our eyes are too busy searching for things we *think* will infuse hope: financial security, makeovers, losing weight, marriage, a new baby. But these are only Band-Aids. Our *true* hope is in Christ alone.

*Lord, all those things are good, and they do give us hope
temporarily. But it's a hope for today only, a hope that
will not last into eternity. We thank You for the never-ending
hope that is always right before us when we look into
the loving, waiting face of our Savior. Amen.*

PRUNE JUICE, ANYONE?

Therefore, with minds that are alert and fully sober,
set your hope on the grace to be brought to you
when Jesus Christ is revealed at his coming.
1 PETER 1:13 NIV

Diets are the devil. They exclude chocolate éclairs and hinge on effective use of that dreaded *s* word: *self-control*. In the fruit bowl of the Spirit, self-control is the prune. It's hard to swallow but nonetheless essential to our faith—especially where hope is concerned. If self-control isn't exercised, we can find our spirits soaring up and down faster than the numbers on our bathroom scales. Like prunes, daily use of self-control regulates us and prepares us for action.

Dear Lord, we long to be controlled by Your Spirit,
not blown about by winds of emotion. Please show us
what that looks like in Your Word and in the lives of
disciplined fellow-believers. We know You long to mature
us in this area: make us moldable in Your hands. Amen.

NO SHAME

No one whose hope is in you
will ever be put to shame.
PSALM 25:3 NIV

Some of us have A-temperaments. We're not quite as flamboyant as type A personalities or as pensive as type B, but because of our tendency to rev our tongues into overdrive before getting our brains in gear, we spend a lot of time extracting foot from mouth. God implores us to control our tongues; the tiny sparks that inflame forests; the rudders that control enormous ships—our means of shame or glorifying His name!

Dear Lord, thank You for Your Word, which reminds
us of the power of the tongue: it can bless or curse,
praise or revile. We pray for the power of Your Spirit
to so revive our hearts that what spills out will be
only things that please You. In faith and hope, amen.

TRUE COLORS

May integrity and honesty protect me,
for I put my hope in you.
PSALM 25:21 NLT

At first the raven appeared solid black, but when she perched in a shaft of sunlight, her feathers shimmered in iridescent emerald, turquoise, and teal: her *true* colors.

We sometimes hide little acts of dishonesty—taking the bank's pen, pocketing that extra dollar from the clerk's mistake, fudging tax figures. But our integrity is on display at all times to the One who gave His life for us. When our true colors are exposed in the Son-light, we want to shimmer too.

Dear Father, help me to act in private as I would act at the foot of Your throne. All my life is as open to You as if I were standing before You. I long to hear You say, "Well done." Help me—sinner though I am—be worthy of those words. Amen.

CREATING A CHALICE

*So we're not giving up. How could we! Even though
on the outside it often looks like things are falling apart
on us, on the inside, where God is making new life,
not a day goes by without his unfolding grace.*

2 CORINTHIANS 4:16 MSG

Okay, so you popped a tire and the boss exploded because you were late for work *again.* Your dog up-chucked in front of the dinner guests. Your daughter failed the big test. Your elderly mother fell and broke her hip. Bill collectors recite your number by heart. That's the outside. On the inside, God is sanding your sharp edges—impatience, frustration, worry—into a smooth chalice filled with His grace.

*Dear Lord, we tend to hate the things that cause us
anxiety and worry, forgetting that You use them to mold
us into the likeness of Your Son. Thank You for the grace
that transforms terrible things into glory. We don't
understand it, but we rest in Your sovereignty. Amen.*

AIM HIGH

*My aim is to raise hopes by pointing
the way to life without end.*
TITUS 1:2 MSG

No woman is an island. We're more like peninsulas. Although
we sometimes feel isolated, we're connected to one another
by the roots of womanhood. We're all in this together, girls. As
we look around, we can't help but see sisters who need a hand,
a warm smile, a caring touch. And especially hope. People
need hope, and if we know the Lord—the source of eternal
hope—it's up to us to point the way through love.

*Dear Lord, we are here on earth to be Your hands and
feet and to point others to the source of our eternal hope.
Open our lives and our lips to speak Your Name. Free us
from fear and the isolation of self-sufficiency. Give us
the grace to help and be helped. Amen.*

JUMP IN

*"You don't need more faith. There is no 'more' or
'less' in faith. If you have a bare kernel of faith,
say the size of a poppy seed, you could say to this
sycamore tree, 'Go jump in the lake,' and it would do it."*
LUKE 17:6 MSG

Luke 17:6 is an intriguing verse. Jesus says there are no increments of faith. You either have it or you don't. Just like you can't be just a little pregnant—you either are or you aren't. Having the faith of Billy Graham or Mother Teresa may seem unfathomable to us, but if we earnestly and completely trust Jesus as our Savior, the Bible says we already do. And God is ready to work through our lives as He has theirs.

*God, we pray, like the father whose son Jesus healed,
I believe; help my unbelief. Help us step out onto the
water of our faith so that we can see that it is already
holding us up. Help us see who the author and perfecter
of our faith is—not ourselves, but You. Amen.*

INTEGRITY

Is not your fear of God your confidence,
and the integrity of your ways your hope?

JOB 4:6 NASB

Live your faith. These three little words are the goal of every Christian. *Not* "Don't smoke, cuss, or chew or hang around with those who do," or even "Be good so you'll get into heaven." Integrity begets behavior, not the other way around. We want to please our Lord by righteous behavior so we can fulfill the challenge of St. Francis of Assisi: "Preach the gospel at all times. Use words if necessary."

Dear Lord, we pray our lives would be a reflection of our beliefs so the Gospel would not be put to shame. Let us live so that unbelievers are drawn in by the fragrance of Christ and let us always be ready to give the reason for our hope. Amen.

GLORIOUS AWAKENING

I pray that the eyes of your heart may be enlightened in order
that you may know the hope to which he has called you,
the riches of his glorious inheritance in his holy people.

EPHESIANS 1:18 NIV

"Open the eyes of my heart, Lord. I want to see you." The lyrics of this beautiful praise song express our deepest desire— to truly *see* the hope before us. Like stereograms with 3-D images embedded within 2-D pictures (You know, those hidden images you can't see without squinting?) the glory and riches of following Christ are veiled to some because the eyes of their hearts are closed. Let us pray for our own spiritual awakening today.

God, we pray for the eyes of those we love who do not know
You to be opened. Seeing this way isn't natural; it requires
a movement of Your Spirit. Thank You for opening our eyes
when we first believed. Unveil Your glory today, Lord,
in a deeper, truer, more beautiful way. Amen.

MEET ME THERE

Christ gives me the strength to face anything.
PHILIPPIANS 4:13 CEV

Most women dread going out alone—to restaurants, shopping, social events—even church. Sometimes we are the loneliest when we're in a crowd. It's intimidating to face a roomful of strangers. But it's well worth it to bite the bullet and *just go* to that church brunch or spiritual retreat or Bible Study. I would have missed some awesome blessings if I hadn't gone (alone) to many spiritual events. I found I did know somebody after all. Jesus met me there.

Dear Lord, help me get my eyes off myself and on to others and You. Help me forget my discomfort and look for others to encourage and befriend. And I know that in doing so, I will be acting as Your hands and feet to the lonely and the friendless. Amen.

FLY ME AWAY

But those who hope in the LORD will renew their strength.
They will soar on wings like eagles; they will run and
not grow weary, they will walk and not be faint.
ISAIAH 40:31 NIV

On those weary days when our chins drag the ground, when our feet are stuck fast in the quagmire of everyday responsibility, this verse becomes our hope and our prayer: Mount me up with wings like eagles; Father, fly me away! Let my spirit soar above the clouds on the winds of your strength. Make me strong as a marathon runner, continuing mile after mile after mile. Be my tailwind, Lord. Amen.

Dear Father, it's not really another cup of coffee that
I need. I need Your presence. Forgive me for looking to
things outside of You to help me renew my strength.
Only You will help me walk—day in and day out,
into eternity—and not grow weary. Amen.

FILL 'ER UP

*"What strength do I have,
that I should still hope?"*

Job 6:11 NIV

Run, rush, hurry, dash: a typical American woman's day. It's easy to identify with David's lament in Psalm 22:14 (NASB): "I am poured out like water. . .my heart is like wax; it is melted within me." Translation: I'm pooped; I'm numb; I'm drained dry. When we are at the end of our strength, God doesn't want us to lose hope of the refilling He can provide if we only lift our empty cups to Him.

Father, show me what it really looks like to lift my empty cup to You. Please meet me here in this tired, pooped, poured-out place where there is none of me left. I know that when I reach the end of me, I'll find You: my strength, my Rock, my hope. Amen.

REBOOT

Be strong in the Lord and in his mighty power.
Ephesians 6:10 nlt

The toilet overflows, sink regurgitates, check bounces, temper flies, washing machine dances, scale shows a three pound *gain*, kids stampede, husband forgets *again*. . . .

Ever have one of those days? You're at the end of your rope, barely hanging on with clawed fingernails. How marvelous that when we're at our weakest point, our Lord is at His strongest, and He gladly shares that strength with us. He won't necessarily fix the plumbing or rewire the spouse, but He *will* reboot our attitudes.

Lord, sometimes all we have the energy to say to You is "Help!" Please take that desperate, exhausted prayer and magnify it into the patience, peace, creativity, and energy that we need to get through the day, not just by the skin of our teeth, but with grace and love. You are able. Amen.

FEARFULLY MADE

You knit me together in my mother's womb. I praise you because I am fearfully and wonderfully made.
PSALM 139:13–14 NIV

Crow's-feet, frizzy hair, saddle bags, big feet—most women dislike something about their bodies. We feel much more fearfully than wonderfully made. But God loves us just as we are. He wants us to look past the wrinkles and see laugh footprints; to use those knobby knees for praying and age-spotted hands for serving. And in the process, praise Him for limbs that move, eyes that see, and ears that hear His Word.

Dear Father, we are Your beloved children. We know we don't (usually) walk around fuming about our own children's flaws and inabilities; the simple fact that they are ours makes them beautiful. You see us like that too, beloved Father. Thank You for creating and delighting in us. Amen.

LAUGH A RAINBOW

*"When I see the rainbow in the clouds, I will
remember the eternal covenant between
God and every living creature on earth."*

GENESIS 9:16 NLT

Ever feel like a cloud is hanging over your head? Sometimes the cloud darkens to the color of bruises, and we're deluged with cold rain that seems to have no end. When you're in the midst of one of life's thunderstorms, tape this saying to your mirror: *Cry a river, laugh a rainbow.* The rainbow, the symbol of hope that God gave Noah after the flood, reminds us even today that every storm will eventually pass.

*Dear Lord, thank You for Your precious promises which
sustain us when deep waters threaten to overwhelm us.
Help us to hold on to them like life preservers. We praise You
for the approaching day when Your Son—the Light of the
World—will burn away every storm cloud forever. Amen.*

More Inspiration for Your Heart

Nevertheless, She Prayed

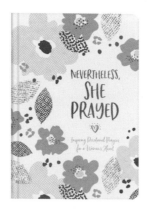

Nevertheless, She Prayed is a lovely devotional prayer collection designed to help you grow deeper in your faith and connect to your heavenly Father's heart. Dozens of practical and encouraging prayers inspired by Ephesians 1:15–23 will help you celebrate the beautiful gift of prayer and strengthen your heart-connection to the Master Creator. You will discover a deeper understanding and love for the One who holds the whole world in His hands.

Hardback / 978-1-64352-407-8 / $14.99